NATIONAL ACADEMIES Sciences Engineering Medicine

NATIONAL ACADEMIES PRESS
Washington, DC

Assessing NASA Science Activation 2.0

Progress, Achievements, and Strategic Recommendations

Margaret Honey, Wendy Gram, and
Kenne Dibner, *Editors*

Committee to Assess NASA
Science Activation 2.0

Board on Science Education

Division of Behavioral and Social
Sciences and Education

Consensus Study Report

NATIONAL ACADEMIES PRESS 500 Fifth Street, NW Washington, DC 20001

This activity was supported by contracts between the National Academy of Sciences and the National Aeronautics and Space Administration (80HQTR22DA001/80HQTR23FA005). Any opinions, findings, conclusions, or recommendations expressed in this publication do not necessarily reflect the views of any organization or agency that provided support for the project.

International Standard Book Number-13: 978-0-309-72749-5
International Standard Book Number-10: 0-309-72749-9
Digital Object Identifier: https://doi.org/10.17226/27989

Cover image credit: NASA, ESA, CSA, STScI, Webb ERO Production Team.

This publication is available from the National Academies Press, 500 Fifth Street, NW, Keck 360, Washington, DC 20001; (800) 624-6242; http://www.nap.edu.

Printed in the United States of America.

Suggested citation: National Academies of Sciences, Engineering, and Medicine. 2025. *Assessing NASA Science Activation 2.0: Progress, Achievements, and Strategic Recommendations*. Washington, DC: National Academies Press. https://doi.org/10.17226/27989.

Consensus Study Reports published by the National Academies of Sciences, Engineering, and Medicine document the evidence-based consensus on the study's statement of task by an authoring committee of experts. Reports typically include findings, conclusions, and recommendations based on information gathered by the committee and the committee's deliberations. Each report has been subjected to a rigorous and independent peer-review process and it represents the position of the National Academies on the statement of task.

Proceedings published by the National Academies of Sciences, Engineering, and Medicine chronicle the presentations and discussions at a workshop, symposium, or other event convened by the National Academies. The statements and opinions contained in proceedings are those of the participants and are not endorsed by other participants, the planning committee, or the National Academies.

Rapid Expert Consultations published by the National Academies of Sciences, Engineering, and Medicine are authored by subject-matter experts on narrowly focused topics that can be supported by a body of evidence. The discussions contained in rapid expert consultations are considered those of the authors and do not contain policy recommendations. Rapid expert consultations are reviewed by the institution before release.

For information about other products and activities of the National Academies, please visit www.nationalacademies.org/about/whatwedo.

COMMITTEE TO ASSESS NASA SCIENCE ACTIVATION 2.0

MARGARET HONEY (*Chair*), President, Scratch Foundation
WENDY GRAM (*Vice Chair*), COMET Deputy Director, University Corporation for Atmospheric Research
FLÁVIO S. AZEVEDO, Associate Professor, Department of Teaching & Learning, Simmons School of Education and Human Development, Southern Methodist University
PAULA BONTEMPI, Dean of the Graduate School of Oceanography, University of Rhode Island
ORLANDO FIGUEROA, Founder, Orlando Leadership Enterprise
ROGERS P. HALL, Wachtmeister Family Professor of Education, Emeritus, Vanderbilt University
VICTOR R. LEE, Associate Professor, Stanford Graduate School of Education
ALINA MARTINEZ, Former Principal Researcher and Director, Mathematica
RAJUL PANDYA, Professor of Practice, Mary Lou Fulton Teachers College, and Executive Director, Global Futures Education Lab, Arizona State University
DARRYL N. WILLIAMS, Senior Vice President, Science and Education, The Franklin Institute

Staff

KENNE DIBNER, Study Director
JANET GAO, Program Officer
LUCY OLIVEROS, Senior Program Assistant
HEIDI SCHWEINGRUBER, Board Director, Board on Science Education

BOARD ON SCIENCE EDUCATION

Reviewers

This Consensus Study Report was reviewed in draft form by individuals chosen for their diverse perspectives and technical expertise. The purpose of this independent review is to provide candid and critical comments that will assist the National Academies of Sciences, Engineering, and Medicine in making each published report as sound as possible and to ensure that it meets the institutional standards for quality, objectivity, evidence, and responsiveness to the study charge. The review comments and draft manuscript remain confidential to protect the integrity of the deliberative process.

We thank the following individuals for their review of this report:

BRONWYN BEVAN, Vice President, Research, The Wallace Foundation
KEVIN BONINE, Undergraduate Research and Scholar Development, Undergraduate Education, Office of the Provost, The University of Arizona
GUDIEL R. CROSTHWAITE, Superintendent, Lynwood Unified School District, CA
KAREEM EDOUARD, Department of Teaching, Learning, and Curriculum, School of Education, Drexel University
CAITLIN FARRELL, National Center of Research in Policy and Practice, School of Education, University of Colorado
ANDRES HENRIQUEZ, STEM Education Strategy, U.S. Division, Education Development Center
CHRIS IMPEY, Department of Astronomy, The University of Arizona

Although the reviewers listed above provided many constructive comments and suggestions, they were not asked to endorse the conclusions or recommendations of this report nor did they see the final draft before its release. The review of this report was overseen by **MICHAEL C. LACH,** Superintendent, Hinsdale High School District 86, IL, and **KATHERINE H. FREEMAN,** Department of Geosciences, Pennsylvania State University. They were responsible for making certain that an independent examination of this report was carried out in accordance with the standards of the National Academies and that all review comments were carefully considered. Responsibility for the final content rests entirely with the authoring committee and the National Academies.

Acknowledgments

This Consensus Study Report reflects the invaluable contributions of many individuals who provided their expertise, including those who served on the committee; the staff of the National Academies of Sciences, Engineering, and Medicine (National Academies); and many other experts who participated in the committee's discussions.

This report was made possible by sponsorship from the National Aeronautics and Space Administration (NASA). We first thank Kristen Erickson, former Director of Science Engagement and Partnerships with NASA Science Mission Directorate; and Lin Chambers, Science Activation Project Manager, for requesting the study and providing ongoing insight to the committee. The Board on Science Education (BOSE) is deeply grateful for our decade-long partnership with Science Activation.

Over the course of the study, the committee held public information-gathering meetings, and committee members greatly benefited from presentations by, and discussions with, the participating individuals: Steve Rider, Pacific Research and Evaluation; Kristi Manseth, Pacific Research and Evaluation; Taline Kuyumjian, Pacific Research and Evaluation; Ben Hamlington, NASA's Jet Propulsion Laboratory; Carl Lewis, Fairchild Gardens; Sue Allen, Allen & Associates; Dennis Schatz, Pacific Science Center; Jackie DeLisi, Education Development Center; Eric Banilower, Horizon Research; and Colleen Manning, Goodman Research Group. The committee is also deeply grateful to the principal investigators, project staff, and project participants from the following SciAct projects, who generously shared their time and insight on our multiple site visits: NASA HEAT, the Gulf of Maine Research Institute, Astronomy Activation Ambassadors, NASA

Community College Network, NASA Night Sky Network, Navigating the Path of Totality at the Exploratorium, NASA's Neurodiversity Network, and Native Earth | Native Sky.

We are also grateful for the efforts of Daniel Aguirre, who prepared a brief background paper synthesizing learnings from our site visits for use in drafting the report.

Thanks are also due to project staff. Janet Gao (Program Officer, BOSE) provided critical assistance by helping with report production. Heidi Schweingruber (Director, BOSE) remains the lynchpin of BOSE: her wisdom, insight, and endless support are the key to BOSE's success. Lucy Oliveros (Senior Program Assistant, BOSE), in her first consensus study with BOSE, deftly managed the study's complicated logistical and administrative needs and assisted with manuscript preparation.

Finally, we thank Kirsten Sampson Snyder (Director of Reports, Division of Behavioral and Social Sciences and Education) for expertly guiding us through the National Academies review process and for unending patience in moving this project along.

Contents

Preface xv

Summary 1

1 **Introduction** 7
THE COMMITTEE'S CHARGE AND APPROACH, 8
EVIDENCE GATHERING AND SITE VISITS, 10
GOALS FOR THE REPORT, 11
ORGANIZATION OF THE REPORT, 12

2 **Background and Context** 13
HISTORY AND CHARACTERIZATION OF THE SCIENCE ACTIVATION PROGRAM, 13
CONTEXT OF THE SCIENCE ACTIVATION PROGRAM WITHIN NASA AND COMPARED WITH SIMILAR FUNDING PROGRAMS, 16
NATIONAL STEM EDUCATION LANDSCAPE, 17
SUMMARY, 22

3 **Evolution: SciAct 1.0 to SciAct 2.0** 23
CHANGES IN RESPONSE TO EARLIER NATIONAL ACADEMIES RECOMMENDATIONS, 23
THE CURRENT PORTFOLIO: SCIACT 2.0, 33
DEFINING SUCCESS FOR SCIACT 2.0, 41

4 **Considerations for SciAct 3.0** 45
EXPERTISE AND THE ROLE OF NASA ASSETS, 45
LEARNING ECOSYSTEMS WITHIN THE SCIENCE ACTIVATION PORTFOLIO, 48
EXPANDING COMMUNITY-CENTERED APPROACHES, 51
MEETING THE UNIQUE NEEDS OF SPECIFIC PROJECTS, 54
THE POTENTIAL OF PROFESSIONAL LEARNING IN SCIENCE ACTIVATION, 57
SUMMARY, 62

5 **Recommendations for SciAct 3.0** 65
OPPORTUNITIES FOR IMPROVEMENT: INTENTIONAL COMMUNICATION, 65
COMMUNICATING SCIENCE ACTIVATION IMPACTS AND RELEVANCE ACROSS NASA AND BEYOND, 66
FINAL THOUGHTS AND RECOMMENDATIONS, 67

References 73

Appendix A Input for the Committee 79

Appendix B Committee Members' Biographies 81

Boxes and Figures

BOXES

1-1 Charge to the Committee, 9

3-1 Science Activation Mid-Level Objectives, 25

FIGURES

3-1 Science Activation's model, emphasizing collaboration with NASA and among Science Activation projects, 35
3-2 Science Activation 2.0 portfolio-level logic model, 40

Preface

NASA's Science Activation program (SciAct) represents a rich and diverse body of work, and it has been a rare privilege to follow its growth and evolution over a 10-year period. As we reflect on a decade of science engagement, learning, and innovation, the accomplishments of SciAct projects are a testament not just to the vision and dedication of the teams involved but also to the collaborative spirit that defines the work.

At the heart of SciAct's success are the countless individuals, organizations, and communities that have committed to making the program's vision a reality. To all the scientists, educators, learners, and advocates who have engaged with and supported SciAct, your enthusiasm and commitment have been a constant source of inspiration. Your efforts to promote discovery and learning across diverse communities will continue to grow the program's reach and depth, ensuring SciAct's impact on millions of people across the country.

We also extend our deepest appreciation to our colleagues at NASA, whose commitment to scientific excellence and engagement is unparalleled. The collaborative models and partnerships fostered through this program not only have advanced STEM education but have significantly advanced the cause of STEM learning and engagement for the nation.

Finally, we wish to thank our insightful and generous colleagues who agreed to volunteer their time and expertise to serve on the committee and shape this report. Your rigorous review and discerning recommendations not only will help to shape the future of SciAct but will guide the program toward even greater impact.

We thank you all for your many contributions to this endeavor.

With gratitude,

Margaret Honey, *Committee Chair*
Wendy Gram, *Committee Vice Chair*
Kenne Dibner, *Study Director*

Summary

The Science Activation program (SciAct) is a $50 million cooperative agreement-making program established in 2015 as part of the National Aeronautics and Space Administration's (NASA's) Science Mission Directorate (SMD). SciAct currently funds 37 active education and engagement projects across the country. Since its inception, SciAct has successfully engaged a diversity of audiences in NASA science. In 2019, NASA commissioned a National Academies of Sciences, Engineering, and Medicine review of the SciAct portfolio, which summarized the program's progress in meeting its original objectives and provided recommendations for strengthening future work. In response to that report, SciAct made considerable changes to its structure and operation to support its second cycle of funding, known colloquially as SciAct 2.0.

In 2024, SciAct is now nearing the end of its second funding cycle and is poised to deepen its commitment to the nation by reflecting on the successes of the past few years and addressing persistent challenges. To inform future SciAct programming, NASA tasked the National Academies' Board on Science Education (BOSE) with conducting a second review of the SciAct portfolio. In response, BOSE convened the Committee to Assess Science Activation 2.0, which included 10 individuals with expertise in Earth science, planetary science, collaborative models and partnerships, collective impact, education policy, community engagement, and learning and teaching in science and engineering. Over a period of 12 months, the committee gathered evidence from oral testimony, interviews, site visits, and review of documentation. The committee's final report provides a comprehensive review of the SciAct 2.0 portfolio and offers recommendations for improvement. The report also provides documentation of the unique value of SciAct both within NASA and for external audiences. Finally, it offers insight into a successful, federally funded, collaborative model for supporting science, technology, engineering, and mathematics (STEM) education and engagement.

EVOLUTION OF SCIACT 2.0

The primary objectives of SciAct involve leveraging NASA's science content, data, and experts to "connect NASA science with diverse learners of all ages in ways that activate minds and promote a deeper understanding of our world and beyond,"[1] namely to

- Enable STEM education;
- Improve U.S. scientific literacy;
- Advance national education goals; and
- Leverage efforts through partnerships.

SciAct describes projects in the portfolio using a small set of categories: SMD division, audience age, educational setting, and delivery model. The committee found that SciAct projects can also be characterized by length and depth of participant engagement, as well as by nature of the engagement strategy (i.e., traditional dissemination approaches or community-centered approaches).

In response to the recommendations in the 2020 National Academies assessment, SciAct made several changes. Notable achievements include the following:

- Continuing to connect individuals with science through SciAct project activities.
- Creating a diverse portfolio of projects that
    - Are designed for NASA outreach and intentional participant engagement;
    - Represent the full spectrum of disciplines embodied by SMD's divisions;
    - Include a wide range of learners and activities;
    - Focus on broadening participation of groups historically underrepresented in SMD STEM fields; and
    - Reach learners across U.S. states and territories and beyond.
- Better leveraging NASA assets including SMD experts, science discoveries, and SMD resources.

[1] https://science.nasa.gov/learn/about-science-activation/

- Establishing successful partnerships, including those that represent a diversity of engagement modes ranging from dissemination approaches to community-engagement approaches.
- Within individual projects, enhancing use of evidence-based and best-practice approaches that support learning and emphasize learner- and community-centered instructional design and practices.
- Engaging a portfolio-level evaluator intended to assess impact across the entire SciAct program.

CONSIDERATIONS FOR SCIACT 3.0

Five areas could be considered for the next phase of programming—SciAct 3.0: (1) deepening the recognition and utilization of expertise throughout the portfolio, (2) considering how learning ecosystems are supported and leveraged, (3) improving and expanding community-centered approaches, (4) meeting the unique needs of specific projects, and (5) enhancing the professional learning community of SciAct awardees.

Expertise and the Role of NASA Assets

NASA is a valuable and distinguished national resource for innovative scientific expertise, evidenced by broad public excitement around NASA's newest discoveries and products and enthusiasm for NASA scientists as participants in SciAct-related events. Scientific expertise is a crucial resource for the entire SciAct portfolio, and numerous NASA assets and experts play vital roles in current SciAct projects. The design of SciAct 3.0 presents an opportunity to more clearly, and potentially more broadly, define NASA assets and expertise, particularly in light of embracing community-centered approaches.

Supporting Projects with a Learning Ecosystems Approach

The 2020 National Academies assessment of SciAct introduced the concept of a "learning ecosystem," which involves the diverse settings in which learning experiences can take place as well as the variety of individuals participating in those experiences. Projects with compelling learning ecosystems are often characterized by the involvement of multiple institutional venues or types and the unique assets of those venues, as well as by active collaboration between sites, which contributes site-specific expertise that can boost the overall success of the learning ecosystem. Creation of a learning ecosystem is time-intensive work, and it is important to account for the learning ecosystem's stage of development during evaluations.

Expanding Community-Centered Approaches

SciAct 2.0 has evolved to include more projects that are co-designed and led with communities, focus on broader community outcomes, and contribute to community scientific literacy. Many projects include communities whose members have historically been underrepresented in science and/or whose knowledge has historically been underappreciated in mainstream science. Such projects offer lessons that can help NASA engage more effectively, and such lessons can enrich all component projects of the SciAct portfolio. Key areas of learning from community-focused projects include strategies for advancing diversity, equity, inclusion, and accessibility; improving community scientific literacy and agency; and expanding SciAct's understanding of expertise. Several SciAct projects include goals that emphasize community service, community value, and good community relationships. However, concerns exist regarding possible tension between NASA's dissemination goals and projects' goals of serving communities.

Meeting the Unique Needs of Specific Projects

The SciAct 2.0 portfolio varies across several dimensions—geography, discipline, formal or informal settings, age groups, and partners. SciAct 2.0 projects vary by depth/breadth of engagement and nature of the engagement strategy (i.e., dissemination driven versus community centered). This diversity helps SciAct address its objectives, promotes learning from multiple methodologies and modalities, and can create a diverse STEM learning ecosystem. Realizing this potential, however, necessitates attention to the unique needs of specific project types, frameworks that coordinate work across projects and promote cross-project learning, and a transparent vision of overall SciAct success that helps clarify projects' potential contributions to that vision. In the years since the 2020 National Academies assessment, the literature around broadening participation has expanded substantively to offer deeper insight into achieving various equity aims. For this reason, it is particularly important to provide tailored support for projects focused on SciAct's broadening participation goals.

Enhancing the Professional Learning Community Among SciAct Awardees

SciAct has the potential to develop its existing network structures into a professional learning community, in which individual project teams can better build and share knowledge across the SciAct portfolio. Creating time and space for knowledge sharing and professional learning community development requires that SciAct inventory the various goals projects are pursuing, assess where and how project team members gain professional knowledge relevant to the development and implementation of SciAct programs, and consider how NASA could provide infrastructure to support multiple points of contact with valuable knowledge. For many project teams, particularly those established in SciAct 1.0, the SciAct community is an excellent source of ideas, collaborators, learning, and connections to NASA assets and expertise. However, committee discussions with some SciAct project leadership, particularly those from projects that were more recently added to the SciAct portfolio, found that SciAct does not appear to provide adequate support or infrastructure for project staff to truly access these resources. Providing ongoing support for cross-project learning could further amplify meaningful collaboration across projects, learning from other projects' successes and challenges, and identifying project-appropriate subject matter experts or scientific assets.

RECOMMENDATIONS

The committee is duly impressed by SciAct's progress since the 2020 National Academies assessment: not only has SciAct acted upon every recommendation outlined in the first report, but the program has also taken additional steps to support the projects in its portfolio. In the wake of this second assessment, we identified a suite of recommendations that, if implemented, can further propel SciAct toward meeting its goals. These recommendations are intended to capitalize on the ongoing work of SciAct, in support of furthering the program's considerable progress.

Recommendation 1: SciAct should be transparent about the goals of its portfolio evaluation and clear about its intentions for using evaluation results. Furthermore, in light of the portfolio's diverse nature, the evaluation should consider measuring SciAct's impact through multiple measures instead of a single measure. To capture the breadth and depth of project work, the portfolio-level evaluation should utilize methods that highlight stories and narratives of learning and change.

Recommendation 2: In building the next iteration of its portfolio, SciAct should consider further investment in community-centered approaches to programming. In expanding this investment, SciAct should ensure that future funded projects attend to modes of engagement and learning that center community-engaged approaches.

Recommendation 3: As SciAct continues its commitment to broadening participation, it should develop strategies for engaging with audiences and communities that have been historically excluded from NASA and

science generally, and place priority on (1) supporting existing projects that include those groups and (2) expanding the number of projects that work with those populations.

Recommendation 4: SciAct should refine its logic model to reflect the theoretical underpinnings and theories of change by which program and project inputs and activities are expected to lead to desired outcomes, particularly with respect to community-centered approaches in which communities may set priorities and outcomes.

Recommendation 5: Given the importance of leveraging NASA assets for meeting the goals of SciAct, SciAct should clarify its definition of subject matter expertise. Specifically, while all projects require subject matter expertise, only some projects will leverage NASA subject matter experts (SMEs) as an identified NASA asset. SciAct should specify what is meant by SMEs and use that definition when building a portfolio that balances multiple types of asset use.

Recommendation 6: SciAct should continue to build on the network structures that have been created, and develop those structures in a professional learning community, such that separate project teams can better generate and share knowledge across projects in the SciAct portfolio.

1

Introduction

The historic accomplishments of National Aeronautics and Space Administration (NASA) science live large in the imaginations of individuals around the world: in 2023 alone, over 380 million fans and followers engaged with NASA's ongoing scientific findings and technological advances through NASA's 15 social media accounts. The NASA "brand" remains one of the most recognizable in the world, rivaling widely known corporate names such as Coca-Cola and Apple. NASA is known across the globe for its ambitious science, technology, and engineering goals: from space exploration to revolutionizing weather prediction to using satellite technology to help farmers plan for shifts in growing seasons, NASA's list of accomplishments is unparalleled. These awe-inspiring achievements give the public a window into the possibilities presented through science, technology, and engineering. By and large, people share deep affection for NASA's impressive moments of discovery and innovation.

To serve the public and respond to financial and sentimental investments in the agency, NASA continuously funds communication and education efforts designed to engage the public in learning about NASA science.[1] The Science Activation program (SciAct) is one such ongoing investment. SciAct, part of NASA's Science Mission Directorate, is a $50 million per year program tasked with funding education and engagement projects around the country. Since its inception in 2015, SciAct has successfully engaged diverse audiences in NASA science to enhance learning in science,

[1] This sentence was changed after release of the report to better reflect NASA's education goals.

technology, engineering, and mathematics (STEM) and to increase participants' engagement with NASA's work. In 2019, NASA commissioned a National Academies of Sciences, Engineering, and Medicine (National Academies) review of the SciAct portfolio,[2] which assessed the history, status, and vision of the program and its projects and provided recommendations for strengthening future work. In response to that report, SciAct considerably changed its structure and operation during its second cycle of funding, known colloquially as SciAct 2.0.[3]

SciAct is now nearing the end of its second five-year funding cycle and is poised to deepen its commitment to the nation by reflecting on recent successes and addressing persistent challenges. A few salient questions emerge: Is SciAct positioned to leverage the best evidence on education and learning to inform its programming? How can SciAct deepen its relationship with the communities it serves? Is SciAct reaching the right audiences, and which communities are currently underserved in SciAct 2.0?

To address these questions, NASA tasked the National Academies' Board on Science Education (BOSE) with conducting a second review of the SciAct portfolio. In response to NASA's request, BOSE convened the Committee to Assess Science Activation 2.0 (see Box 1-1 for the committee's charge). The 10-member committee included individuals with expertise in Earth science, planetary science, collaborative models and partnerships, collective impact, education policy, community engagement, and learning and teaching in science and engineering (see Appendix B for biographical sketches). This report provides a comprehensive review of SciAct 2.0 and offers additional recommendations for improving the program.

THE COMMITTEE'S CHARGE AND APPROACH

A preliminary conversation with project sponsors helped to define the scope of the committee's work. First, this assessment is not designed to evaluate the effectiveness or success of SciAct. Per the recommendations in the first National Academies' report on this topic, *NASA's Science Activation Program: Achievements and Opportunities* (NASEM, 2020; hereafter referred to as "the 2020 National Academies assessment"), SciAct hired a portfolio evaluator, whose ongoing role is to determine how well SciAct is meeting its stated objectives. The committee's job was to consider

[2] The committee uses the term "program" to signal an organized funding stream designed to meet specific goals. The term "portfolio" is used to describe the suite of individual projects funded by SciAct.

[3] Throughout this report, SciAct 1.0 is used to refer to the first iteration of the program (2015–2020); SciAct 2.0 refers to changes made since the 2020 National Academies assessment (2021–2025); and SciAct 3.0 refers to future work to be undertaken following the current assessment.

BOX 1-1
Charge to the Committee

An ad hoc committee of the National Academies will assess the National Aeronautics and Space Administration (NASA) Science Mission Directorate (SMD) Science Activation (SciAct) program's current efforts, in its second phase, towards meeting its four stated top-level objectives and corresponding mid-level objectives in support of SciAct 2.0's overarching vision and desired outcomes. Objectives of the SciAct program are: enable STEM education, improve U.S. scientific literacy, advance national education goals, and leverage efforts through partnerships. Particular areas of interest are in broadening participation of lifelong learners with NASA subject matter experts and authentic experiences.

The National Academies committee will carry out its work by drawing on: (1) evidence about effective STEM education in and out of school summarized in previous reports from the Board on Science Education, (2) documentation of changes to the SciAct program since the National Academies' 2020 Science Activation assessment, and (3) knowledge of SMD science content from the Space Studies Board. The committee's final report will:

- Provide a concise written assessment of the status of the SMD SciAct program, including discussion of the revisions made since the 2020 National Academies assessment;
- Identify any gaps in the SciAct approach, given new advances in science education pedagogy and recent decadal recommendations; and
- Make recommendations related to management of and priorities for the next phase of the program (SciAct 3.0).

whether SciAct is organized to effectively leverage current knowledge about supporting science engagement and learning in various contexts and the emerging insights from projects in the SciAct portfolio. In short, the committee was tasked with assessing SciAct's structure and operation rather than its outcomes.

Furthermore, this report does not endorse or critique the individual efforts of the 37 SciAct projects but rather considers how SciAct can organize and support its projects to enhance the aggregate impact of the portfolio. As noted in the 2020 National Academies assessment, SciAct's cooperative agreement process affords opportunities for funding of projects that have a clearly articulated, narrow focus but do not address every objective in the Cooperative Agreement Notice (see NASEM, 2020, Chapter 3). Through funding a diverse portfolio of projects, SciAct seeks to leverage the focused expertise of individual projects to yield a set of collective resources and opportunities that together respond to the needs of the education community and of learners, are scientifically accurate, are grounded in current education research, and are deeply aligned with science and engineering practices. The current committee's attempts to characterize overall trends in the portfolio are intended to identify gaps in SciAct's approach related to the structure and operation of the program and are not meant as a critique of any individual project.

Lastly, the committee considered areas of interest highlighted in the charge "broadening participation of lifelong learners with NASA subject matter experts and authentic experiences." Specific to NASA subject matter experts (SMEs), the committee continually revisited the question of how projects are leveraging SMEs throughout their work: our observations and recommendations on this topic are embedded throughout the report. Regarding the objective of "authentic experiences," the committee engaged in several early conversations around the meaning of "authentic" and how projects could assess whether their work was providing learners with authentic opportunities to participate in science. We declined to specifically define "authentic" for each and every project in the portfolio, but as we will discuss in Chapter 4, we recognize that authentic experiences are often contingent on the extent to which learners can bring their own cultures, perspectives, and concerns into their participation. We discuss ways to deepen learners' connections to science through community approaches to programming in Chapter 4.

EVIDENCE GATHERING AND SITE VISITS

The committee used several mechanisms for gathering information to inform this review. First, we held multiple open-session conversations with members of the SciAct portfolio, as well as with experts on various aspects of STEM education and engagement. In the first committee meeting, Kristen Erickson (Director, Science Engagement and Partnerships at NASA Science Mission Directorate) provided a comprehensive overview of SciAct's history, its efforts to reorganize, and the status of the portfolio. Erickson was supported by Lin Chambers (SciAct Integration Manager, now SciAct Project Manager). In subsequent meetings, several SciAct awardees, as well as portfolio- and individual project-level evaluators shed light on their experiences (see Appendix A for a list of open-session presenters).

Second, several committee members attended the 2023 annual meeting of SciAct principal investigators, where we held a town hall-style event and small-group breakout sessions to gather the perspectives of meeting participants and to determine the type of guidance that would be most useful for SciAct 3.0. Committee members in attendance also had the opportunity to hold informal conversations with SciAct investigators and NASA staff.

Third, the committee conducted multiple site visits and observations of funded projects in the spring of 2024 as part of its evidence-gathering processes (see Appendix A for a list of projects visited). These site visits were invaluable for our work: each visit provided direct insight from project stakeholders on the successes and challenges faced in their work. Furthermore, site visits deepened our understanding of how well SciAct is positioned to support the diverse needs of its individual projects—findings that will be discussed throughout this report. Site visits were not included as part of the information gathering during the 2020 National Academies assessment.

Finally, in addition to evidence gathered through oral testimony, the committee reviewed documentation of program progress provided by SciAct, including SciAct's 2020 and 2021 Research Opportunities in Space and Earth Sciences (ROSES)[4] solicitations (see Chapter 2), annual reports for all 37 projects, SciAct's 2022 and 2023 annual reporting documents, as well as materials furnished by SciAct's portfolio-level evaluator, Pacific Research and Evaluation.

GOALS FOR THE REPORT

This report responds to a request from SciAct itself and serves to support the program in its aim to operate at its full potential and meet its stated goals, in the interest of maximizing U.S. taxpayers' investment in NASA. The report serves three main purposes: (1) to assist SciAct leadership[5] in making programmatic changes to improve program effectiveness; (2) to communicate the unique value of SciAct, both to NASA and to external audiences; and (3) to provide the field of science education with insight into a federally funded, collaborative model for supporting STEM education and engagement. SciAct has unique potential to leverage NASA's considerable assets to meet the needs and concerns of STEM learners and communities around the country, and this report aims to support that effort. In reviewing the documentation of programmatic changes made following the 2020 National Academies assessment, the committee observed multiple improvements that can serve as learning opportunities for the broader science education community: of particular note is SciAct's considerable investment in

---

[4] The ROSES solicitation tool is the primary mechanism through which NASA issues requests for proposals to support research and programming. The 2020 and 2021 SciAct ROSES calls can be found here: https://nspires.nasaprs.com /external/solicitations/summary!init.do?solId=%7B1FB5B0CC-E90C-F0A0-BC4C-6F8D9DD1A3EC%7D&path=open and https://nspires.nasaprs.com/external/solicitations /summary!init.do?solId=%7B70022F64-A0FD-0B3D-7FFA-FCC298C068E6%7D&path=open, respectively.

[5] Throughout the report, "SciAct leadership" refers to the leadership and administrative staff employed by NASA to implement the SciAct portfolio.

supporting a robust learning community across funded projects. Thus, this report documenting SciAct's progress can provide other federal agencies and funders with insights that could inform improvements of their own programs.

ORGANIZATION OF THE REPORT

Chapter 2 provides an overview of the historical and programmatic background of SciAct and offers insight into critical issues that have emerged or shifted in the STEM education landscape since the 2020 National Academies assessment. Chapter 3 discusses SciAct's evolution since the 2020 National Academies assessment and characterizes the SciAct 2.0 portfolio. This appraisal sets the stage for the next two chapters: Chapter 4 provides a suite of considerations for SciAct leadership in their planning for SciAct 3.0, and Chapter 5 concludes the report with a set of recommendations for SciAct's future.

2

Background and Context

To make clear recommendations for the future of the Science Activation program (SciAct), the committee first acknowledged the need to understand SciAct's considerable history, as well as the context in which it currently operates. This chapter offers a brief programmatic history of SciAct and briefly describes the current SciAct 2.0 portfolio. We then turn to a description of the current national STEM education landscape to contextualize our recommendations for SciAct's next iteration.

HISTORY AND CHARACTERIZATION OF THE SCIENCE ACTIVATION PROGRAM

SciAct was established in 2015 as part of National Aeronautics and Space Administration's (NASA's) Science Mission Directorate (SMD), "to connect NASA science with diverse learners of all ages in ways that activate minds and promote a deeper understanding of our world and beyond."[1] The current top-level objectives of SciAct were established at that time:

- Enable STEM education;
- Improve U.S. scientific literacy;
- Advance national education goals; and
- Leverage efforts through partnerships.

---

[1] https://science.nasa.gov/learn/about-science-activation/

SciAct emerged as a new model in the agency to promote and support effective engagement of STEM learners of all ages with SMD science projects by leveraging NASA's science content, data, and experts (i.e., NASA-funded scientists and engineers). The first SciAct portfolio (SciAct 1.0) consisted of 27 projects that were funded for five years (2015–2020), via a competitive, stand-alone Cooperative Agreement Notice (CAN). In 2019, NASA asked the Board on Science Education at the National Academies of Sciences, Engineering, and Medicine (National Academies) to review the SciAct 1.0 portfolio and make recommendations to improve the program as it entered its second funding cycle. To this end, the committee that authored the 2020 National Academies assessment (NASEM, 2020) identified 15 conclusions and made 7 recommendations for SciAct 2.0 (see Chapter 3 for more detail about the 2020 National Academies assessment). In 2020, informed by the 2020 National Academies assessment, SciAct extended 18 SciAct 1.0 projects for an additional five years via a second competitive CAN, creating SciAct 2.0 (2021–2025); 9 of the original 27 projects did not continue to receive funding into SciAct 2.0. Three of the projects that were extended from SciAct 1.0 ended in 2022.

SciAct also invited additional teams to propose projects to complement continuing SciAct 2.0 projects via the Research Opportunities in Space and Earth Sciences (ROSES) omnibus solicitation (ROSES-2020 E.6 Science Activation Program Integration). The ROSES-2020 solicitation highlighted two specific foci for new projects. These foci were informed by the 2020 National Academies assessment:

- Engaging subject matter experts (SMEs), especially NASA employees and NASA-funded SMEs, with learners, content producers, and audience-focused disseminators within the SciAct portfolio.
- Broadening participation of underrepresented and underserved learners to maximize advancement of knowledge.

Nine additional projects were added to the SciAct 2.0 portfolio via the ROSES-2020 solicitation. To further address SciAct priority areas, a second ROSES solicitation (ROSES-2021 F.6 Science Activation Program Integration[2]) was released in 2021, with specific focus areas including the following:

- Heliophysics content, including the annular (2023) and total (2024) solar eclipses.
- Dissemination of SMD assets (i.e., science content and data, space and airborne platforms, and scientific and technical personnel) into communities or specific audience networks.

[2] https://nspires.nasaprs.com/external/solicitations/summary!init.do?solId=%7B70022F64-A0FD-0B3D-7FFA-FCC298C068E6%7D&path=open

- Integration of data into science learning, in alignment with SMD's Strategy for Data Management and Computing for Groundbreaking Science,[3] and NASA's Science Data Overview.[4]

The ROSES-2021 competition resulted in 13 additional SciAct 2.0 cooperative awards to projects around the country.

The SciAct 2.0 portfolio includes 37 active projects that vary in science content area, audience, educational setting, and delivery model, as well as the specific top-level and mid-level program objectives addressed (NASA, n.d.). SciAct 2.0 projects engage a range of audiences, with some serving broad audiences through science centers, mobile applications/websites, citizen science, and libraries; others focus on topics such as professional development for educators across a variety of formal and informal education settings, learning experiences and/or curricula for students, engagement workshops for planetary science SMEs, or bringing oceanography and STEM opportunities to Hispanic/Latinx communities through internship programs. SciAct 2.0 principal investigators (PIs)[5] come from colleges/universities (n = 17), non-profit organizations (n = 13), NASA centers (n = 4), and informal science institutions (n = 3; i.e., museums, science centers, and botanic gardens).

In addition to the above-named projects, SciAct 2.0 also funds 13 NASA-led projects called infrastructure projects, which CAN/ROSES-funded SciAct projects are encouraged to leverage in their work when possible and as appropriate. Infrastructure projects represent an array of organizations and types of public engagement, including the Global Learning and Observations to Benefit the Environment (GLOBE),[6] Night Sky Network,[7] NASA Astro Camp,[8] and Astronomy Picture of the Day.[9] SciAct provides at least some funding for each of these infrastructure projects, commensurate with their role/applicability to SciAct objectives. Most infrastructure projects have been active for decades and are stand-alone projects outside of SciAct. Although infrastructure projects are considered part of SciAct, they are not expected to leverage NASA assets the same way traditionally funded SciAct projects do.

---

[3] https://smd-cms.nasa.gov/wp-content/uploads/2023/04/KnezekSDMWGStrategyUpdate-toAPACMarch2020.pdf

[4] https://science.data.nasa.gov/nasa-science-data-overview/

[5] Throughout the report, "SciAct PIs" refers to the principal investigators leading the individual projects that comprise the SciAct portfolio.

[6] https://www.globe.gov/

[7] https://nightsky.jpl.nasa.gov/

[8] https://www.nasa.gov/stennis/stem-engagement-at-stennis/nasa-accp/

[9] https://apod.nasa.gov/apod/astropix.html

It is important to note that SciAct is designed to function as a *network* of projects: that is, after awards are made, projects are encouraged to collaborate and learn from one another, leverage one another's strengths, and generally cohere in support of the portfolio's goals. NASA intends SciAct programming to take a "collective impact" approach: by building a portfolio comprised of unique but complementary projects, SciAct can leverage synergies across the suite of projects to better meet its objectives. The function of this network has evolved over time, largely in response to the 2020 National Academies assessment's recommendations (see Chapter 3 for discussion of those recommendations and SciAct's response).

CONTEXT OF THE SCIENCE ACTIVATION PROGRAM WITHIN NASA AND COMPARED WITH SIMILAR FUNDING PROGRAMS

As noted above, SciAct is located in NASA's SMD and is separate from the four programs housed in NASA's Office of STEM Engagement (OSTEM).[10] While run entirely independently of SciAct, OSTEM's strategic goals are complementary to SciAct's top-level objectives. OSTEM's goals include the following:[11]

- Attract diverse groups of students to STEM through learning opportunities that spark interest and provide connections to NASA's mission and work.
- Create unique opportunities for a diverse set of students to contribute to NASA's work in exploration and discovery.
- Build a diverse future STEM workforce by engaging students in authentic learning experiences with NASA's people, content, and facilities.

In general, OSTEM programs focus on attracting and preparing students for the STEM workforce, whereas SciAct prioritizes collaborative projects that leverage NASA assets to further STEM education and scientific literacy broadly. Another primary difference between OSTEM and SciAct is that SciAct has intentionally created a collaborative learning community of projects, aiming to collectively achieve desired SciAct outcomes.

SciAct also differs from other federally funded STEM education programs at science agencies. The National Science Foundation (NSF), for example, provides substantial funding for STEM education through

[10] OSTEM includes Next Gen STEM, National Space Grant College and Fellowship Project, Established Program to Stimulate Competitive Research, and Minority University Research and Education Project; https://www.nasa.gov/learning-resources/internship-programs/

[11] https://www.nasa.gov/learning-resources/stem-engagement/

programs such as the Innovative Technology Experiences for Students and Teachers,[12] NSF Discovery Research PreK–12,[13] and NSF Advancing Informal STEM Learning (AISL).[14] However, unlike SciAct, these programs are primarily designed to fund research projects. They also fund a broad array of topics in STEM, in contrast to SciAct's focus on NASA-related science.

The National Oceanic and Atmospheric Administration's portfolio of education programs more closely resembles SciAct's portfolio; however, it does not employ a "collective impact" approach. Indeed, SciAct's collective impact approach stands out among STEM education funding programs in federal agencies: although NSF's Eddie Bernice Johnson Inclusion across the Nation of Communities of Learners of Underrepresented Discoverers in Engineering and Science Initiative[15] also adopted a collective impact model, its focus is primarily on transforming education and career pathways to broaden participation in science and engineering rather than on connecting learners to the science assets of the agency.

NATIONAL STEM EDUCATION LANDSCAPE

To provide SciAct with guidance to inform the future portfolio, the committee considered trends in the current STEM education landscape that intersect with SciAct priorities and that could inform improvements. We identified three key areas in which new developments in STEM education are relevant to SciAct: equity in STEM education, insights from STEM education research, and the evolving nature of the science/research enterprise. In the sections below, we discuss the latest developments in each of these areas and consider implications for SciAct.

Expanding Notions of Equity in PreK–12 STEM Education and Learning

As discussed in Chapter 3, one of the major themes of the 2020 National Academies assessment was SciAct's commitment to "broadening participation," or improving equitable involvement in STEM learning and engagement opportunities. Many of the 2020 National Academies assessment's recommendations focused on this theme, and SciAct made a series of choices to support broadening participation efforts (see Chapter 3 for discussion of SciAct's response to the 2020 National Academies assessment). Since 2020, however, the field of education has changed dramatically

[12] https://new.nsf.gov/funding/opportunities/itest-innovative-technology-experiences-students-teachers

[13] https://new.nsf.gov/funding/opportunities/drk-12-discovery-research-prek-12

[14] https://new.nsf.gov/funding/opportunities/aisl-advancing-informal-stem-learning

[15] https://new.nsf.gov/funding/opportunities/nsfs-eddie-bernice-johnson-inclusion-across-nation

in terms of "broadening participation" in STEM. Broadening participation, which involves increasing the demographic diversity of STEM participants, is now seen as an aspect of the larger goal of achieving equity in STEM learning experiences.

The shift toward a focus on equity rather than on increasing demographic diversity (i.e., counting the number of people from certain backgrounds enrolled in a program) has emerged from the recognition that historical underrepresentation of select demographic groups in STEM results from deep structural inequities in both the education system and in STEM workplaces. A variety of factors shape individuals' access to STEM education and engagement opportunities and their subsequent experiences. Working toward equity illustrates a recognition of the multiple barriers that might block people from pursuing STEM fields and the related structural and programmatic changes that could promote the success of STEM learners regardless of their backgrounds.

This consideration of equity has been taken up across the broader STEM education community; however, relevant to this report, what would it mean for SciAct to pursue equity goals? In 2024, education policymaking demands a sophisticated, multi-layered understanding of equity and what enacting equity looks like. To support SciAct in understanding how to pursue equity, the committee consulted *Equity in K–12 STEM Education: Framing Decisions for the Future* (NASEM, 2024).

Equity in STEM education is not a singular goal but an ongoing process requiring intentional decision making and action toward addressing and disrupting existing inequities and envisioning a more equitable future. Given the specific histories and contexts of various schools, districts, communities, regions, and STEM education generally, equity-related goals and strategies for achieving them may vary substantially and may also change over time.

For SciAct, this means that education decision makers (i.e., SciAct leadership, SciAct PIs, and SciAct project staff[16]) have the opportunity to interpret and enact decisions to advance equity in their programs in ways that reflect the priorities of SciAct's leadership, project leaders and staff, and the learners and communities with which SciAct engages. Steps toward equity in SciAct will necessitate an understanding of the policies, key actors, and potential resources within each individual project context, to support each project's specific equity goals. Simultaneously, consequential decision making for increasing equity at both the portfolio and individual project levels involves helping SciAct leadership and project staff balance short-term gains with a vision for, and strategic action toward, long-term and

[16] Throughout the report, the term "project staff" refers to staff members employed by individual projects in the SciAct portfolio.

continuous change. In SciAct 2.0, different stakeholders employ different ways of thinking about equity in STEM education. A clear, consistent vision for an equitable SciAct will help SciAct leadership and project staff realize SciAct's equity goals and will help orient ongoing design and implementation decisions toward meeting those goals.

Equity in K–12 STEM Education: Framing Decisions for the Future also identifies a series of equity frames to help decision makers articulate short- and long-term equity goals and make policy and practice decisions (NASEM, 2024). By viewing these decision-making frames in concert, it is clear that pursuing equity in STEM goes beyond expanding access to STEM education opportunities. Rather, equity work often involves addressing programming content, as well as considering how individual and community participants understand themselves in relationship to STEM. In short, to pursue equity goals, SciAct leadership and project staff will greatly benefit from a clear vision for a future equitable project or portfolio. Chapter 4 considers how SciAct leadership might help projects leverage community-based approaches to support both portfolio- and project-level equity goals.

Insights from STEM Education Research

A major focus of the 2020 National Academies assessment was the importance of centering evidence-based approaches to STEM learning in the design and implementation of both individual SciAct projects and the portfolio as a whole. The 2020 National Academies assessment described a suite of research-based STEM learning principles (NASEM, 2020, pp. 56–63). The 2020 committee identified three principles of STEM learning as critical to SciAct's work:

- Proficiency in STEM disciplines goes beyond simply learning content. Instead, it involves engaging people with the practices, language, and tools of the discipline (NASEM, 2018a).
- Research demonstrates that learners' interests, experiences, and concerns play pivotal roles in motivating their decisions to participate in learning activities (NASEM, 2018a).
- STEM learning occurs across a broad constellation of settings, timeframes, and experiences (National Research Council, 2006, 2009), often referred to as the STEM learning ecosystem.

Since the National Academies 2020 assessment, additional evidence on supporting STEM learning has emerged, and this evidence can be leveraged to support SciAct. For example, *Science and Engineering in Preschool Through Elementary Grades: The Brilliance of Children and the Strengths of Educators* (NASEM, 2022) focused on strengthening STEM education experiences in younger grades. That report posited four "big ideas" to help conceptualize STEM learning: (1) learning is a social and cultural process; (2) learning involves identity formation; (3) learning occurs across cultural contexts; and (4) teaching and learning are not "neutral" because they are shaped by social and political forces. The report posits that these four ideas are central to understanding both the core commonalities and the broad variations in how individuals learn.

This committee noted that the importance of identity formation is missing from the discussion of STEM learning in the 2020 National Academies assessment of SciAct. Indeed, research increasingly demonstrates that STEM learning is inextricably linked to participants' identities—that is, whether participants see themselves as able to do STEM, see their communities as valuable to STEM, and see their communities represented in STEM knowledge generation (Nolen et al., 2011; Oyserman & Destin, 2010). Ultimately, how and what participants learn relates to how they see themselves, the kinds of people they want to become, and the people they can be in learning contexts (Hand & Gresalfi, 2015).

> Viewing learning as identity formation means that science and engineering educators' work is to nurture *humans*, not only to nurture humans' *minds*. Science and engineering identity development have been documented among elementary-aged youth (Kane, 2012; Tai et al., 2006) and even among younger children in their play choices (Rowe & Neitzel, 2010) and in the kinds of science or engineering engagement families provide (Pattison et al., 2020). In a study of 58 amateur adult astronomers and 49 birders, Jones and colleagues (2017) found that many hobbyists' lifelong science interests began in childhood, shaped by family members and the social capital they provided through science-related leisure activities. Lifelong learning in these hobbies is an indicator of sustained science identity work (Bell et al., 2012). (NASEM, 2022, p. 61)

Supporting STEM learning is central to SciAct's mission: indeed, three of SciAct's top-level objectives involve supporting participants' learning in STEM (i.e., enable STEM education, improve U.S. scientific literacy, and advance national education goals). Expanding access to programming is not enough to further these top-level objectives: as the 2020 National Academies assessment notes, the design and implementation of meaningful learning opportunities requires SciAct leadership and project staff to explicitly determine how to engage and support all participants in their learning experiences. Given the role that identity formation plays in supporting both engagement in and learning from STEM experiences, the committee recognizes that identity formation is in fact a central tenet of meeting the three STEM learning goals identified above. For more on the role of identity in supporting participants' STEM learning experiences, see Chapter 4.

Expanding Considerations of Science

In considering how to support SciAct's continued development, the committee held the grounding assumption that, at its core, SciAct aims to help the public connect with and engage in the U.S. scientific enterprise. Thus, it is important for SciAct to consider the changing nature of this enterprise as the scientific community increasingly recognizes the importance of connecting with and learning from non-scientists, valuing diverse expertise, and working in collaboration with local communities.

Federal investment in scientific research and education increasingly emphasizes impactful and equitable societal outcomes (Berhe, 2023; Brenninkmeijer, 2022; NASA, 2023b; National Institutes of Health, 2023; National Science Foundation, 2022). Calls for community-engaged scientific research have increased—that is, research that brings together policymakers, researchers, community leaders, and others who collaborate to identify evidence needs, combine diverse forms of knowledge and expertise, and use evidence to accomplish shared goals. Across disciplines, a growing number of scholars is entering academia to affect societal change, often through policy or community partnerships (Finnerty et al., 2024; Villegas et al., 2007).

Both historically and in the current sociopolitical context, societally impactful, community-engaged research broadens participation in knowledge production (Stoecker, 2003), bridges the gap between research and practice (Balazs & Morello-Frosch, 2013), and leverages research to advance social justice (Tuck & Guishard, 2013). "Public scholarship" promotes similar goals, by "generating, transmitting, applying, and preserving knowledge for the direct benefit of external audiences in ways that are consistent with University and unit missions" (Michigan State University, 1993, p. 13). Community-engaged research can be identified by five main approaches:

1. *Dialogue and deliberation*: Public discussion and deliberation regarding the intersection of societal issues with science, technology, and innovation.
2. *Community-driven citizen science*: Projects that address community interests and questions using research approaches co-developed by non-professional scientists.
3. *Civic engagement and policymaking*: Projects that use research as an input for collective action and policy and governance decisions to advance communities' goals.
4. *Open innovation*: Open challenges, competitions, and calls to action that use science and technology to solve difficult problems.
5. *Participatory research*: Community participation in the design and implementation of research initiatives (Association of Science and Technology Centers, 2024).

Given SciAct's commitment to connecting the public with NASA science and the powerful role that communities can play in supporting science learning and engagement, the committee recognizes the importance of helping SciAct develop effective, mutually beneficial approaches to future work with communities. Chapter 4 discusses how SciAct can employ community-based approaches to meet its fourth objective, leveraging efforts through partnerships, as well as to support projects currently engaged in community-facing work.

SUMMARY

This chapter describes the status of SciAct 2.0, along with the STEM education background and context within which SciAct 2.0 exists. As noted above, the 37 SciAct 2.0 projects cover vastly different science content areas, types of participants, educational settings, and delivery modes. As discussed in Chapter 3, each of these 37 projects is designed to pursue one or more of nine programmatic objectives, and each project exists against the evolving backdrop of science and education in the United States.

With this landscape in mind, the committee identified three key areas in which new developments in STEM education are relevant to SciAct: equity in STEM education, insights from STEM education research, and the evolving nature of the science/research enterprise. Since the 2020 National Academies assessment, research has developed in relationship to the term "broadening participation," and education scholarship has codified four "big ideas" for understanding how individuals learn in STEM: (1) learning is a social and cultural process; (2) learning involves identity formation; (3) learning occurs across cultural contexts; and (4) teaching and learning are not "neutral" because they are shaped by social and political forces. Lastly, we discussed the changing nature of the scientific research enterprise as the scientific community increasingly recognizes the importance of connecting with and learning from non-scientists, valuing diverse expertise, and working in collaboration with local communities. Overall, this chapter sets the stage for the committee's assessment of SciAct 2.0: by understanding both the programmatic history of SciAct, as well as the current landscape of STEM education, we can orient our recommendations for SciAct 3.0.

3

Evolution: SciAct 1.0 to SciAct 2.0

This chapter describes the evolution of the Science Activation program (SciAct) 1.0 in response to recommendations in the National Academies of Sciences, Engineering, and Medicine's (National Academies') report *NASA's Science Activation Program: Achievements and Opportunities* (NASEM, 2020), noting specific successes and programmatic challenges as well as highlighting potential opportunities for improvement. The chapter then describes the SciAct 2.0 portfolio in depth, including a discussion of SciAct's new portfolio-level evaluation, and summarizes the committee's understanding of SciAct 2.0's successes.

CHANGES IN RESPONSE TO EARLIER NATIONAL ACADEMIES RECOMMENDATIONS

As noted previously, the 2020 National Academies assessment of SciAct found that, although the program had successes during the first five-year period (SciAct 1.0), additional refinements and steps could be taken to better fulfill the program's overall goals. To this end, the committee outlined a suite of specific recommendations for SciAct 2.0. Within each of the sections that follow, we describe SciAct's progress in addressing each recommendation from the 2020 National Academies assessment, and we identify opportunities for additional progress, which informed our recommendations for SciAct 3.0.

Refining SciAct's Focus

2020 Recommendation 1: SciAct should go through a visioning process that brings the portfolio up to date with current research on learning and design, the new federal STEM plan, and evidence-based approaches to broadening participation. This process should also consider how SciAct fits within and contributes to the larger STEM education ecosystem and should provide the foundation for developing actionable and measurable portfolio goals.

2020 Recommendation 2: SciAct should articulate how it expects that the portfolio will leverage NASA assets, how partnerships and networks will be built, and how these actions will lead to desired, measurable outcomes.

Response to Recommendations

In response to these recommendations, SciAct embarked on a visioning process. Activities at the 2019 and 2020 annual meetings involved SciAct projects in this process. Through visioning activities conducted in collaboration with SciAct grantees, SciAct developed specific, concrete program objectives that could be incorporated into individual project objectives. Activities included conversations with principal investigators (PIs) in fall 2019, a workshop to identify and define mid-level objectives (MLOs), and a conversation open to SciAct PIs and project staff to discuss the operationalization of those objectives. This process resulted in a set of MLOs that fall under each of SciAct's top-level objectives (see Box 3-1).

Project PIs and their project-level evaluators are tasked with identifying the MLOs that are most salient for their projects and including these MLOs in their evaluation plans. The portfolio-level evaluator (described later in this chapter) has engaged in efforts to understand how SciAct projects are incorporating MLOs, and has identified MLOs 1a, 1b, and 3b as the most pursued MLOs. The committee sees the inclusive process for developing the MLOs and their adoption by projects as responsive to 2020 Recommendation 1 and notes many project-level staff told the committee that the MLOs were helpful as they defined their individual project-level goals and focused their programmatic efforts.

Opportunities for Improvement

Further specifying the portfolio's desired outcomes is a key opportunity. Although both SciAct leadership and portfolio-level evaluators developed distinct program logic models to illustrate the theory of change

BOX 3-1
Science Activation Mid-Level Objectives

1. Top-level objective—Enable STEM education
   Mid-level objectives:
   a. Inspire participants' interest in STEM and the development of their identities as science learners.
   b. Provide opportunities for participants to engage with discipline-specific content related to NASA science and engineering.
   c. Increase the number of NASA Science Mission Directorate (SMD) assets used by learners across the United States, and the frequency with which they are used.
2. Top-level objective—Improve U.S. scientific literacy
   Mid-level objective:
   a. Advance participants' understanding of science and its processes using NASA SMD assets.
3. Top-level objective—Advance national education goals
   Mid-level objectives:
   a. Increase participation in learner-centered experiences based on NASA SMD assets.
   b. Increase the diversity of participants reached by SciAct through intentional, inclusive programming.
   c. Engage participants in learning experiences that promote development of skills for STEM careers.
4. Top-level objective—Leverage efforts through partnerships
   Mid-level objectives:
   a. Leverage internal mechanisms to support sharing and learning across the SciAct portfolio.
   b. Utilize external partners to leverage reach and effectiveness of the SciAct portfolio.

SOURCE: National Aeronautics and Space Administration. (2023). *NASA's 2023 equity action plan.* https://assests.performance.gov/cx/equity-action-plans/2023/EO_NASA_EAP_2023.pdf

underlying the program (see discussion later in this chapter), neither model clearly identifies specific, measurable portfolio-level outcomes or outputs. Therefore, the committee observed an existing opportunity for SciAct to further clarify its vision for how chosen inputs and activities will produce desired results. We discuss how SciAct might approach this opportunity in Chapter 5.

Development of a Coordinated Learning Network

2020 Recommendation 3: SciAct must consider whether the development of a coordinated learning network of awardees across its portfolio is a program priority. If it is a priority, then the program must provide the necessary infrastructure to support a more active network of projects. At the very least, SciAct needs to develop more systematic mechanisms for projects to share best practices and learn from successes and failures.

Response to Recommendation

Following the release of the 2020 National Academies assessment, SciAct leadership identified the learning network concept as a priority in the program's conceptual framework and took several steps to make this priority salient and to provide the infrastructure to support it. To support a learning network, the program has invested in several areas:

- Creation of additional staff positions to provide support for collaboration across SciAct and with other National Aeronautics and Space Administration (NASA) programs.
- Establishment of monthly meetings, action groups, and support for building new communities of practice, to support internal sharing and learning within the SciAct network.
- Selection of tools and activities that enable knowledge sharing.
    - In fall 2020, a research team at the Massachusetts Institute of Technology[1] was selected to help SciAct leadership understand the community of SciAct projects, including an analysis of partnerships[2] leveraged across the portfolio.
    - Action groups, many of which were co-designed at SciAct's annual meetings, were formalized to support cross-project collaborations around key program priorities, including
        - Broadening participation,
        - Process of (doing) science,
        - Citizen science,
        - Digital learning,
        - James Webb Space Telescope action group,
        - Indigenous community relationships,
        - Women and girls,

[1] https://science.nasa.gov/sciact-team/mit-media-lab/, Dr. Rachell Connolly (PI).

[2] https://science.nasa.gov/learn/leverage/

        - Data visualization,
        - Data fluency/open science, and
        - Diversability.[3]
    - Some action groups have evolved into communities of practice or affinity groups, each with their own goals and activities, including
        - Holding monthly meetings to share successes and challenges,
        - Providing educational sessions across SciAct projects,
        - Publishing peer-reviewed papers,
        - Sharing resources, and
        - Developing recommendations for SciAct projects and leadership.
- Points of contact (POCs) have been identified within each SMD science division, to serve as internal ambassadors for SciAct. These POCs presented on their division's current missions and recent advances at SciAct's 2023 annual meeting.

Based on committee members' conversations with grantees, efforts to strengthen connections across projects in the portfolio and to enhance opportunities for grantees to learn from each other have been positively received and are useful. These activities, which serve to build out the learning network of grantees, are a major advancement of SciAct 2.0.

Additionally, SciAct issued new solicitations (the Research Opportunities in Space and Earth Sciences [ROSES] 2020 call discussed in Chapter 2) encouraging projects that would address gaps in the portfolio identified in the National Academies 2020 assessment. In response to the recommendation related to developing a coordinated learning network, SciAct STEM Ecosystems[4] was selected from SMD's ROSES-2020[5] grant solicitation to support the development of a network across SciAct projects and to view the portfolio through the lens of a STEM education ecosystem. SciAct STEM Ecosystems convened a meeting in early 2024, which brought together individuals from about 40 SciAct projects. SciAct STEM Ecosystems also conducted an inquiry to explore ecosystem best practices within SciAct. SciAct leadership has been explicit that its programmatic investments are small relative to the investments made in STEM education across the United States. Thus, SciAct looks for leverage points to capitalize on NASA assets—the agency's content, data, brand, and the excitement of subject matter experts (SMEs).

---

[3] The term "diversability" is used by SciAct in relationship to supporting diversity among learners.

[4] https://science.nasa.gov/sciact-team/stem-ecosystems/

[5] https://science.nasa.gov/researchers/solicitations/roses-2024/research-opportunities-in-space-and-earth-science-roses-2024-to-be-released-february-14-2024/

Opportunities for Improvement

While SciAct projects appear to value the regular check-ins and opportunities to collaborate, some SciAct PIs and project staff expressed the desire for additional opportunities for intentional collaboration. At the same time, some projects indicated limited bandwidth and resources to collaborate. Chapter 4 discusses how SciAct might consider expanding opportunities for projects to learn from one another.

Filling SciAct Portfolio Gaps

2020 Recommendation 4: SciAct should use the opportunity provided by Phase Two to reflect on the current portfolio within the context of the new vision, goals, and logic model. This process should critically review and guide existing projects, be explicit about the rationale and criteria for including new projects, and consider how best to integrate them into the existing portfolio. One important area for consideration is how to ensure that underserved communities receive more focused attention in the next phase of the program.

Response to Recommendation

As part of reviewing the existing portfolio and deciding how to build out the portfolio of projects for SciAct 2.0, SciAct implemented a competitive process to review extension plans submitted by SciAct 1.0 projects. In addition, the ROSES-2020 solicitation (see Chapter 2 for details of this solicitation) was explicit about two specific focus areas: (1) ways that NASA SMEs could engage with the projects, and (2) efforts to broaden participation of underrepresented and underserved learners. A subsequent "gap-filling" ROSES-2021 solicitation was released to cover three focal areas: (1) heliophysics content, (2) dissemination of SMD assets into communities or specific audience networks, and (3) integration of data in science learning. In the committee's judgment, the SciAct 2.0 portfolio successfully included projects that purposefully involve a diverse set of learners and communities (areas of interest for both ROSES-2020 and ROSES-2021). Eighteen of the 37 non-infrastructure projects in the SciAct 2.0 portfolio focus on specific underserved audiences, including Native American nations in five states, learners on the autism spectrum, people who are blind or have low vision, Black and Latinx communities, and community college students.

The purposeful expansion of the portfolio with careful review of existing projects and use of ROSES competitions to intentionally fill identified gaps has resulted in a stronger portfolio and is very responsive to 2020 Recommendation 4.

Opportunities for Improvement

Given the strong community formed among existing SciAct projects, embracing new projects often required intentional effort. Bringing additional projects into the SciAct community for SciAct 3.0 will likely also require explicit attention as new personnel and partners become involved.

Deepening Commitment to Broadening Participation

2020 Recommendation 5: SciAct should deepen its commitment to broadening participation by using evaluation measures that go beyond counting numbers of individuals who represent specific groups. In order to do this, SciAct must identify ways that the portfolio as a whole could draw upon and implement evidence-based strategies for broadening participation.

Response to Recommendation

The ROSES-2020 solicitation's emphasis on broadening participation resulted in several proposals that articulated plans to work deeply and strategically with groups that are traditionally underrepresented and underserved in STEM. Through a peer-review process, SciAct selected a number of these projects for inclusion in SciAct 2.0, and, as noted in the previous section, the committee views this expansion of the audiences served by projects within the portfolio as a positive step forward.

SciAct is also working to provide support for projects that are engaging with groups that have been traditionally underserved and underrepresented in STEM. A monthly learning community, one of the activities of the Broadening Participation action group, supports sharing of diversity, equity, inclusion, and accessibility (DEIA) expertise across projects by featuring a presentation in each virtual meeting, during which a project team shares insights into their successful DEIA efforts.[6]

Project-level evaluations of projects working in partnership with communities include documentation and examination of how projects are involving and engaging communities. In some projects, these efforts include capturing how SciAct teams incorporate traditional, Indigenous, and ecological knowledge. Also, some formative evaluations are capturing how

[6] This sentence was changed after release of the report to correct an error regarding the origin of the Broadening Participation action group.

projects are engaging in a co-design process with community members and are feeding that information back to project PIs to help improve their efforts, as well as sharing learnings with the broader SciAct community. This knowledge sharing has occurred at large meetings, and it is also described in the 2022 *NASA Science Activation Impact Report*; however, it is unclear the extent to which this is documented in proposal narratives or project annual reports, as well as how this has been actualized and measured within and across projects.

SciAct projects also engage in internal discussions around DEIA to further share learnings from work with specific demographic groups. In addition to informal sharing of challenges and successes, DEIA-focused sessions were convened at both the annual meeting and education ecosystem meetings.

SciAct has recognized the need to deepen the knowledge of grantees and SciAct staff around supporting DEIA and working with communities. Portfolio expansion offers an opportunity for SciAct to continue to deepen this work. The efforts of project-level evaluators to document partnerships and co-design processes could inform portfolio-level evaluations. These developments are all responsive to 2020 Recommendation 5.

Opportunities for Improvement

An opportunity exists for SciAct to be more intentional, across its portfolio, to include a balance of both learner- and community-centered approaches, as well as to more deeply support community-centered approaches already operating within projects. Chapter 4 discusses potential opportunities for NASA to further expand and deepen its DEIA work beyond its current "broadening participation" approach. Specific to the evaluation component of 2020 Recommendation 5, which called for SciAct to use measures that go beyond "counting numbers of individuals who represent specific groups," Chapter 4 describes how SciAct might more comprehensively represent its successes and challenges by engaging with more narrative, qualitative approaches to evaluation.

Dialogue with Missions and Scientists

2020 Recommendation 6: SciAct should build ongoing opportunities for dialogue with NASA Science Mission Directorate's missions and scientists.

Response to Recommendation

As part of implementing SciAct 2.0, in an effort to strengthen connections to SMD's missions and scientists, SMD science division leads were identified as POCs, to facilitate internal NASA communication around SciAct. POCs present their current missions at the annual SciAct meeting, keeping the SciAct community appraised of ongoing SMD activities and assets. SciAct projects also engage with POCs to establish connections with SMD divisions.

Several projects are working explicitly to make connections between SciAct and the larger professional scientific community, both within NASA and beyond. Two of these projects, namely Planetary Resources and Content Heroes[7] and NASA Community of Practice for Education (SCoPE),[8] were funded through ROSES-2020. Further progress on this recommendation is demonstrated by NASA's Universe of Learning[9] project's work with the astrophysics community.

Establishing POCs, involving them in SciAct annual meetings, and supporting projects designed to connect with the space science community are all positive steps forward. Thus, in the committee's view, SciAct has been responsive to 2020 Recommendation 6.

Opportunities for Improvement

In conversations with SciAct project PIs, the committee heard that finding and connecting with SMD SMEs often relied on PIs' existing individual connections, so some projects were more connected than others. Opportunities to continue evolving the ways SciAct staff and SMD POCs connect SciAct project teams with SMD mission teams exist both within NASA and across the scientific community. SciAct could connect more closely with other NASA programs, such as NASA Engages[10] in the Office of STEM Engagement, which is composed of NASA experts who share NASA missions and content at educational, professional, civic, and other public venues.

Expertise and Evaluation

2020 Recommendation 7: SciAct should create an independent mechanism to obtain ongoing, real-time advice from individuals with expertise in learning and design, the larger policy context of STEM education, partnering with local communities, broadening participation in STEM, and science content relevant to the missions of NASA's Science Mission Directorate. Among other responsibilities, these experts should inform the new visioning and planning process.

---

[7] https://science.nasa.gov/sciact-team/planetary-resources-and-content-heroes/

[8] https://science.nasa.gov/sciact-team/smd-community-of-practice-for-education/

[9] https://universe-of-learning.org/home

[10] https://my.nasa.gov/engages/s/

2020 Recommendation 7a: With input from these experts, SciAct should consider whether and how a portfolio-level evaluation could strengthen the focus of the program and ensure that projects in the portfolio are effectively meeting overarching SciAct program goals and objectives.

Response to Recommendations

Following the 2020 National Academies assessment, SciAct leadership invited individuals with scholarly expertise relevant to a suite of content area concerns highlighted in the 2020 report (e.g., evidence-based approaches to STEM education, broadening participation, engaging with neurodiverse learners) to present at SciAct annual and monthly meetings, and SciAct has used other National Academies reports focused on STEM education to guide its work (NASEM, 2016, 2018b, 2022). Authors of the 2020 National Academies assessment and National Academies staff members engaged in the visioning process and helped to develop MLOs. However, there does not appear to be a mechanism for regular infusion of the expertise suggested in 2020 Recommendation 7.

In response to 2020 Recommendation 7a, SciAct carried out a competitive process to engage a portfolio-level evaluator and selected Pacific Research and Evaluation, LLC (PRE) in December 2020. PRE's activities have included developing a portfolio logic model, exploring the use of MLOs across projects, and working to identify shared measures for evaluating programmatic success across SciAct projects. PRE's team has engaged with the independent project evaluators associated with each SciAct project, whose primary role is assessing the project's progress and providing feedback to both SciAct and project leadership to inform ongoing improvements. A working group of project-level evaluators has been established to facilitate sharing of knowledge and best practices between projects, providing another source of information that may inform overarching SciAct program goals and objectives.

Opportunities for Improvement

With respect to 2020 Recommendation 7, opportunities remain for SciAct to develop a mechanism for regularly obtaining outside expertise to supplement the SciAct community's robust internal networks. With respect to 2020 Recommendation 7a, a key opportunity for SciAct moving forward is articulating which measures of programmatic success are important to capture in the portfolio-level evaluation (see discussion of the portfolio-level evaluation below). Opportunities also exist with consideration to the portfolio-level data-collection process, including which questions are asked and how, which data-collection methods are employed, and the differential capacities of expected data collectors (i.e., project teams/evaluators, SciAct staff, PRE).

THE CURRENT PORTFOLIO: SCIACT 2.0

The following sections provide a brief description of the current portfolio (SciAct 2.0), shaped by SciAct's response to the 2020 National Academies assessment, and describe SciAct 2.0's approach to measuring success. This portfolio description is based on annual SciAct Impact Reports from 2022 to 2023 and the 2021 PRE portfolio-level evaluation plan (PRE, 2021).

Describing SciAct 2.0

Annual SciAct Impact Reports provide both a portfolio-level characterization of impacts and accomplishments along with project-level summaries of project goals, audiences, educational settings, delivery models, accomplishments, key partners, and outputs (i.e., numbers of activities, participants, reach, etc.). These reports show that all five SMD divisions are represented in the SciAct 2.0 portfolio (2022/2023):

- Earth science: 11/10 projects
- Planetary science: 3/3 projects
- Heliophysics: 4/4 projects
- Astrophysics: 3/3 projects
- Biological and physical sciences: 1/1 project
- Division cross-cutting: 15/16 projects

Thirty-five of the 37 non-infrastructure SciAct 2.0 projects work with educators and/or students in formal and/or informal educational settings; only the SMD SCoPE and STEM Ecosystems[11] projects engage solely with NASA SMEs or SciAct project team members, respectively. Over 60% of SciAct projects work with formal and/or informal educators, and most projects either engage directly with or develop resources for youth ages 5–17. Two projects specifically engage with undergraduate students or their instructors: Eclipse Ambassadors Off the Path,[12] which trained amateur astronomers and undergraduate students to provide community outreach

[11] https://science.nasa.gov/sciact-team/stem-ecosystems/

[12] https://science.nasa.gov/learning-resources/science-activation/eclipse-ambassadors-off-the-path-reaching-underrepresented-audiences/

during the 2023 and 2024 eclipse events, and NASA Community College Network,[13] which provides community college instructors with resources, a community of practice, and connections with NASA SMEs. Among the 30 projects working in informal education or out-of-school settings, approximately 35% provide citizen science opportunities, 30% share digital learning opportunities, nearly 50% work with science centers/museums, and 30% work with libraries. Projects also involve historically underserved communities: 8 projects include people with differing abilities, 2 projects work with neurodiverse audiences, 25 projects work with communities with diverse racial/ethnic identities, and 18 projects engage with rural communities (PRE, NASA SciAct Portfolio Groupings Public tool, as provided to the committee).

SciAct 2.0's theory of action is a "collective impact, network-of-networks approach" (NASA, 2023a, p. 4). NASA resources and expertise are the inputs in this approach; SciAct projects implement a variety of activities (e.g., workshops, curricula, online educational resources and tools, engagement activities and public events, citizen science programs, communities of practice, learning ecosystems) to engage various audiences to meet a selection of MLOs. Outputs are mostly dissemination oriented, captured through measures of reach (e.g., number of learner interactions by geographic location [NASA, 2023a, p. 5]), collaboration (e.g., number of partnerships with external organizations and/or with other SciAct teams [NASA, 2023a, pp. 6–7]), participation of NASA SMEs (e.g., number of SMEs participating in SciAct activities by geographic location [NASA, 2023a, p. 8]), peer-reviewed publications (NASA, 2023a, p. 9), availability of learning resources (e.g., number of learning resources by NASA science divisions [NASA, 2023a, p. 9]), and broadening participation (e.g., number of projects within specific communities and number of DEIA and belonging topics shared with the SciAct community [NASA, 2023a, p. 10]). The collective impact approach posits that implementation of these SciAct project activities will contribute to meeting the four top-level objectives of SciAct described in Chapter 2 (Figure 3-1).

Dimensions of SciAct 2.0 Portfolio

SciAct 2.0 uses four descriptive categories to characterize and organize its projects (NASA, 2023a):

1. SMD divisions: Astrophysics, biological/physical sciences, Earth science, heliophysics, and planetary science.
2. Audience age: Ranging from 0 years old and up.

[13] https://science.nasa.gov/sciact-team/nasa-community-college-network/

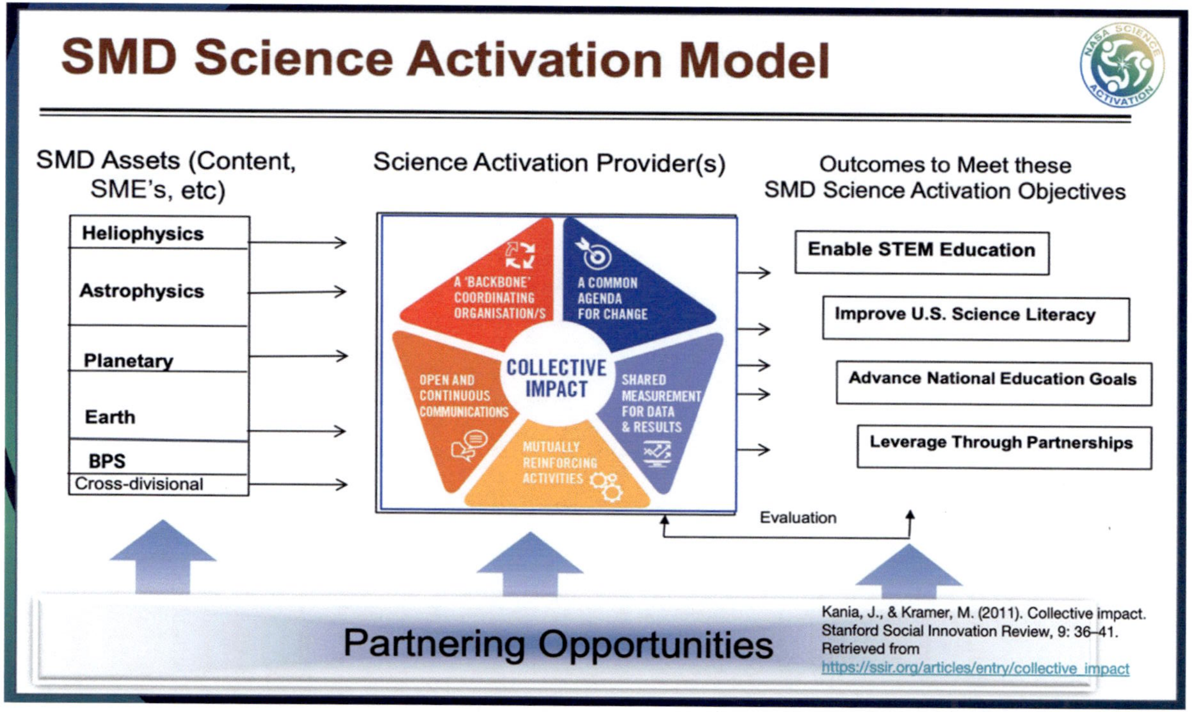

FIGURE 3-1 SciAct's model, emphasizing collaboration with NASA and among SciAct projects.
SOURCES: Lin Chambers, SciAct rep. (November 2023). SciAct annual PI meeting slides; Santo, R. (2019). *Using a collective impact approach to support youth pathways in technology*. New York University. https://digitallearningpractices.org/resource/using-a-collective-impact-approach-to-support-youth-pathways-in-technology

3. Education settings: Informal/out of school, formal education, citizen science, and professional.
4. Delivery models: Independent/self-directed; facilitated learning, guided by informal educators; delivered by formal educators; peer-professional learning.

In addition to these categories, the committee observed that SciAct 2.0 projects could be characterized in two ways that are not currently documented in the 2022 and 2023 Impact Reports: type of engagement and nature of the engagement strategy.

Type of Engagement

SciAct 2.0 contains projects that range in depth of engagement—that is, the length of time participants engage and how deeply they are involved with the scientific ideas and practices. For instance, NASA's Heliophysics Education Activation Team (HEAT)[14] eclipse event, held in Dallas in April 2024, engaged a large number of people in a short-duration interaction. Other activities, like Learning Ecosystems Northeast[15] or the NASA Community College Network, focus on long-term, in-depth interactions with small numbers of people. A spectrum of approaches contributes to a well-functioning science learning ecosystem that supports all learners (Ostman, 2024). For instance, a large science event can be a "spark," generating interest or resources that can be used in many contexts, while long-term events involving the same group of learners allow more time to explore scientific methods and processes. Large-scale dissemination can reach many people who are already inclined toward science, but focused engagement can provide more welcoming environments for nurturing science identity, supporting participants' agency as learners and users of science, and exploring intersectionality of science and culture (Kim & Sinatra, 2018). Research shows that learners benefit from opportunities to connect informal and formal STEM experiences, either through their own choices or via curated pathways, suggesting that the impact of an approach may be multiplied through its connections to other approaches (Hussim et al., 2024). Furthermore, knowledge and products resulting from one approach can inform other approaches—for instance, a curriculum developed with a small group of learners may subsequently be used with a larger group of learners—which is an additional benefit of communication between projects with diverse approaches.

---

[14] https://science.nasa.gov/sciact-team/nasa-heliophysics-education-activation-team/

[15] https://science.nasa.gov/sciact-team/gmri/

Nature of the Engagement Strategy

As discussed in Chapter 2, scientific research in the United States is increasingly leveraging community-oriented approaches. Similarly, SciAct 2.0 projects also span a spectrum of engagement strategies, ranging from projects that are primarily science centered to those that are deeply community centered. Efforts that focus on disseminating science or the "breaking news" of Earth and planetary discovery are on the science-centered end of the spectrum (e.g., eclipse-focused projects, science festivals, opportunities to meet NASA personnel, and educational programs and experiences devoted to missions or topics, like heliophysics). While designers of programs that utlize these approaches often employ knowledge about participants' backgrounds or interests and program activities can be interactive (e.g., a question-and-answer session between participants and astronomers at an eclipse festival), they center scientific content, resources, expertise, and experts. Such approaches can be quite effective for meeting their stated goals: research on festivals, for example, revealed that content-driven approaches can increase participants' interest in science (Illingworth et al., 2015; Jensen & Buckley, 2014) and are particularly attractive if they involve direct interaction with scientists (Boyette & Ramsey, 2019). Dissemination-driven approaches can also increase awareness of science careers (Canovan, 2019; Munn et al., 2018). Moreover, these approaches may amplify the resources present in informal learning institutions, contributing to the overall science ecosystem (Bevc et al., 2016). A weakness of dissemination-driven approaches, however, is that they may primarily attract participants who are more affluent and educated than the general population (Falk & Needham, 2011; Kato-Nitta et al., 2018; Kennedy et al., 2018; Martin, 2017; Nielsen et al., 2019).

Another class of SciAct 2.0 projects focuses on educational opportunities associated with inviting non-scientists to participate in the processes of scientific research, or educational citizen science.[16] SciAct's educational citizen science projects intentionally support participants' learning outcomes as well as participants' scientific contributions, through activities like data collection or image classification. In contrast, other NASA citizen science programs primarily use citizen science as a tool for advancing scientific research, with little focus on participants' learning.

---

[16] The term "citizen science" is problematic, especially in the United States. "Citizen" was originally intended to describe a participant as a "citizen of the world" (Bonney, 2021), but the word may not be welcoming to those living in the United States without documentation (Cooper et al., 2021). "Community science" is sometimes used as a replacement, but in this report, we reserve "community science" for projects that center community knowledge (including knowledge beyond the sciences) and in which community members collaborate to set project priorities, goals, outcomes, and measures.

Educational citizen science projects can afford positive learning outcomes across all strands of individual science literacy (Finger et al., 2023; NASEM, 2018b). Outcomes of educational citizen science projects can be improved by attending to the interests and skills of non-scientist participants (NASEM, 2018b). Educational citizen science projects can provide access to authentic scientific practices that help people understand the intrinsic uncertainty in all scientific work, including that of NASA (Chen et al., 2019; Fischoff & Davis, 2014; Star, 1985). While SciAct can disseminate established scientific information, providing access to authentic scientific practices that manage intrinsic uncertainty is a major opportunity for which educational citizen science is ideally suited.

A similar class of participatory SciAct projects leverages NASA data, people, and assets in ways that are highly relevant in local contexts and represent "science-as-a-service." For example, in the Sea Level Education, Awareness, and Literacy (SEAL)[17] project, NASA SMDs work directly with SMEs who present NASA's satellite-based sea-level data in ways that address local issues and make those data available to local decision makers. In such projects, community priorities drive the overall agenda, which implies a respect for community knowledge. NASA SMEs provide scientific expertise, but community expertise defines pressing needs or issues, such that scientific data, assets, and people can be leveraged in ways that have tangible community impact. As demonstrated by SEAL, science that serves society may be particularly relevant in the face of large-scale community threats like climate change.

In these two kinds of projects—science-as-a-service and educational citizen science—community expertise and leadership play complementary roles. In citizen science, goals are set by scientists, but the interests, skills, and local expertise of community members are critical; in the case of science-as-a-service, scientific expertise is critical, but community goals determine the uses of that expertise.

Finally, some SciAct 2.0 projects intentionally combine community leadership and expertise in both their activities and goal setting, which we will refer to as community approaches to science. In this mode of interaction, science is positioned alongside other types of knowledge, and scientific experts work with community members who bring their own expertise. These efforts often focus on community priorities that include science but extend to issues beyond science. In honoring heterogeneous knowledge systems, such projects often work with cultural communities that have been underserved or even exploited by Western science. For example, Native Earth | Native Sky[18] co-creates culturally relevant Earth

[17] https://science.nasa.gov/sciact-team/seal/

[18] https://science.nasa.gov/sciact-team/native-earth-native-sky/

and sky STEM curricula with three Native American nations in Oklahoma, by interweaving stories, language, and culture into formal classroom Earth and space curricula.

A relationship exists between the various modes of community engagement and the breadth and depth of engagement. Smaller projects tend to be more amenable to community or co-created science or science education, while larger projects necessarily tend to focus on science-centered dissemination strategies. As discussed earlier, these approaches can be connected—a small, focused, in-depth community-science approach could result in curricula well suited for widespread dissemination within relevant communities.

Results from Portfolio-Level Evaluation

NASA SMD selected PRE as the portfolio-level evaluator to help SciAct identify the impact of its portfolio as a collective, and to describe the portfolio's progress in accomplishing its stated objectives (PRE, 2021). As part of this work, PRE developed the following:

- A suite of tools intended to help the SciAct community build a shared understanding of SciAct 2.0 and its component projects, including
  - An MLO Summary Dashboard illustrating the distribution of projects pursuing individual MLOs and project activities designed to meet each MLO;
  - A Measurement Tools Landscape, showing methods projects are using to assess their efforts to address MLOs; and
  - An Audience Dashboard, showing the audience groups with which each project engages.
- A logic model for portfolio evaluation (PRE, 2021; Figure 3-2).
- A suite of common measures to be used across SciAct projects, as appropriate, to understand collective impacts. The recommended common measure, agreed upon at the SciAct annual PI meeting in November 2023, was a single-item measure for assessing STEM identity, called STEM Professional Identity Overlap (STEM PIO-1) (McDonald et al., 2019). This metric is connected to MLO 1a (see Box 3-1); PRE notes that 22 projects in SciAct 2.0 are pursuing MLO 1a as one area of focus.

During 2023, PRE held a series of shared learning sessions with SciAct team members to better understand how MLOs were defined and operationalized across projects. Takeaways from these sessions included the following:

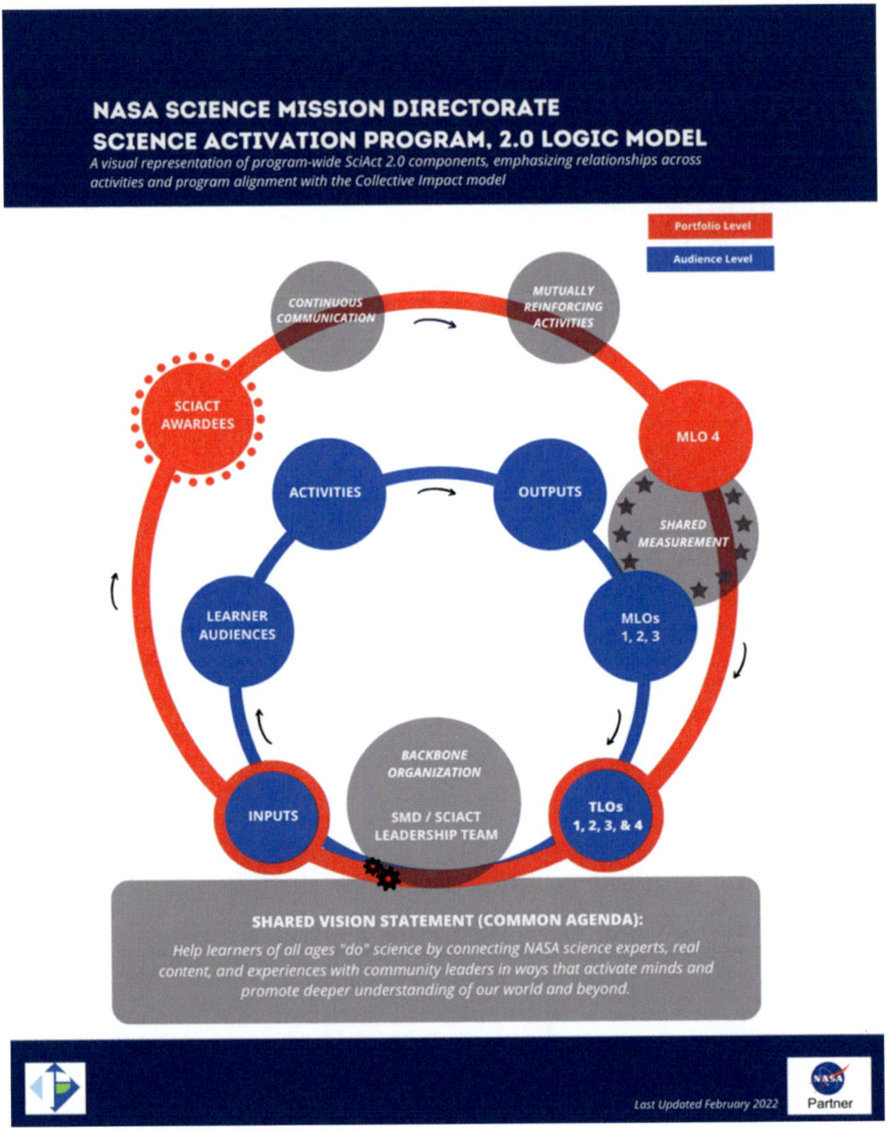

FIGURE 3-2 SciAct 2.0 portfolio-level logic model.
SOURCE: SciAct 2.0 portfolio-level Logic Model, developed by PRE (February 2022).

- Most team members viewed MLO 1b (Provide opportunities for participants to engage with the disciplinary content related to NASA science and engineering) and MLO 1c (Increase number of and frequency with which NASA SMD assets are used by learners across the United States) as project outputs versus outcomes, with a focus on quantifying people, events, or materials or the number of participant engagements with content and/or SMD assets.
- Project staff wanted clarity from SciAct leadership on most MLOs, especially relative to expectations for project reporting and definitions of terms (e.g., "learner," "engagement," and "NASA SMD asset").
- Project staff interpreted MLO 2a (Advance participants' understanding of science and its processes using NASA SMD assets) as focused on learning the process of science, particularly how science is done at NASA.
- Project staff interpreted MLO 3a (Increase participation in learner-centered experiences based on NASA SMD assets) as both an output (e.g., quantifying implementation and engagement by tracking student participation in activities) and, less frequently, as an outcome in which the impact of an activity on participants was assessed. Staff generally expressed that this MLO was easy to understand.
- Project staff appreciated that MLOs were intentionally broad, so as to be applicable to all projects, but staff were unclear on how to report their progress toward MLOs.

DEFINING SUCCESS FOR SCIACT 2.0

SciAct seeks to leverage NASA science content and SMEs to further the understanding and pursuit of science among individuals of all ages. The committee identified several characteristics that demonstrate programmatic "success" for the work accomplished in SciAct 2.0. Although this list is not exhaustive, it represents a suite of achievements that the committee feels signal SciAct 2.0's ongoing progress toward meeting its top-level objectives (see Chapter 2):

- Connecting individuals with science through SciAct project activities.
- Creating a diverse portfolio of projects that
  - Are designed for NASA outreach and intentional participant engagement;
  - Represent the full spectrum of disciplines embodied by SMD's divisions;
  - Include a wide range of learners and activities;

  - Focus on broadening participation of groups historically underrepresented in SMD STEM fields; and
  - Reach learners across U.S. states and territories and beyond.
- Leveraging NASA assets including SMD experts, science discoveries, and SMD resources.
- Establishing successful partnerships, including those that strike a balance between dissemination and community-engagement modes, as described above.
- Using evidence-based and best-practice approaches that support learning across the entire portfolio, emphasizing learner- and community-centered instructional design and practices.

SciAct 2.0 has made observable progress toward meeting its stated objectives: that is, in the wake of the 2020 National Academies assessment, considerable efforts by SciAct leadership and PIs resulted in tangible improvements in the areas listed above. Additionally, these successes can guide potential pathways for a future SciAct 3.0—areas in which SciAct has made changes may serve as instructive examples illustrating how change in the SciAct portfolio happens and where attention is best focused.

The following conclusions summarize the progress of SciAct 2.0.

Conclusion 1: SciAct has made significant progress in response to the recommendations put forth in the 2020 National Academies assessment. Notable achievements include broadening the kinds of communities engaged and creating and sustaining a collaborative network of projects.

Conclusion 2: The creation of mid-level objectives (MLOs) was an important step in clarifying and refining SciAct's goals. Developing MLOs involved collaboration across the entire SciAct portfolio, allowing for input from multiple principal investigators and project staff. While this is a step forward, further refinement of MLOs could help clarify how individual projects could best use/work toward these objectives.

Conclusion 3: The portfolio-wide evaluation, while helpful in many ways to SciAct's administration, favors single metrics (e.g., a survey of science identity) over documenting and describing the successes and challenges of specific awards to capture overall impact and inform progress for the entire portfolio.

Conclusion 4: The current logic model developed by Pacific Research and Evaluation does not clearly identify specific outcomes or outputs, nor does it specify how program and project inputs and activities are expected to lead to desired outcomes.

Conclusion 5: Independent project-level evaluators are an important resource for individual projects and for the overall portfolio. Tailoring evaluations to individual projects captures projects' unique contributions and can inform future work. It is unclear how individual project evaluations inform the portfolio-wide evaluation.

Conclusion 6: SciAct has successfully built a portfolio of projects that are diverse with respect to geographic reach, scientific discipline, types of audiences, and types of partnerships leveraged. The committee noted two additional dimensions represented across projects: deep engagement with a small audience versus lesser-depth engagement with a larger audience, and community-centered approaches versus science-centered approaches.

4

Considerations for SciAct 3.0

Building on the committee's analysis of the evolution of the Science Activation program (SciAct) since the National Academies of Sciences, Engineering, and Medicine's (National Academies') 2020 assessment (NASEM, 2020) described in Chapter 3, this chapter highlights five key areas for future growth of the program: (1) refining approaches to leveraging National Aeronautics and Space Administration (NASA) assets and expertise and recognizing and engaging with various kinds of expertise related to science throughout the portfolio, (2) considering how learning ecosystems are supported and leveraged, (3) improving and expanding community-centered approaches, (4) meeting the unique needs of specific projects, and (5) expanding the potential for professional learning within SciAct. This chapter describes each area, discusses relevant research, and identifies potential directions for the portfolio when planning SciAct 3.0.

EXPERTISE AND THE ROLE OF NASA ASSETS

One hallmark of SciAct that distinguishes it from other federal STEM education programs is the ability to connect with and leverage the unique assets produced by NASA missions. As noted in previous chapters, this includes a wide array of concrete assets (e.g., images, datasets, instruments, and new scientific knowledge) as well as the scientific expertise of NASA scientists and staff. Discussions with grantees and their partners provided insight into the use of assets across projects and pointed to ways that the concept of expertise could be broadened as SciAct deepens engagement with local communities.

Leveraging NASA Assets

As detailed in Chapter 3, SciAct 2.0 utilizes a suite of approaches to leverage NASA's scientific assets, which include the scientific knowledge generated through NASA's missions and the expertise of scientists engaged in NASA's work. NASA is a valuable and distinguished national resource for innovative scientific knowledge and deep scientific expertise, evidenced by broad public excitement around NASA's newest discoveries and products (e.g., images) and enthusiasm for NASA scientists as participants in SciAct-related events. Scientific knowledge and expertise are crucial resources for the entire SciAct portfolio, and NASA assets currently used in SciAct projects include

- Data repositories linked to long-standing mission objectives;
- A sensing and data-gathering infrastructure focused on the dynamics of Earth's atmosphere, land, and waters as well as planetary and deep space exploration;
- Materials developed for STEM learning and teaching (e.g., visualizations, exhibits, and pedagogical activities) using NASA data and supporting infrastructure; and
- A cadre of accomplished subject matter experts (SMEs), who make voluntary contributions to materials development, public outreach, education, and community partnerships.

NASA's infrastructure projects (e.g., Global Learning and Observations to Benefit the Environment [GLOBE], Night Sky Network, NASA Astro Camp) are a type of NASA asset that SciAct projects are encouraged to leverage in their activities and products. As stated in Chapter 2, many infrastructure projects have been active for decades and are stand-alone projects outside SciAct. Some SciAct projects collaborate extensively with an infrastructure project (e.g., Arctic & Earth STEM Integrating GLOBE & NASA [Arctic and Earth SIGNs][1] leverages GLOBE for much of its work), whereas other SciAct projects are not engaged with infrastructure projects.

NASA assets and experts already play a unique and central role in SciAct. However, as SciAct 3.0 is designed, there is an opportunity to more clearly define NASA assets and expertise. The committee noted considerable confusion among principal investigators (PIs) regarding the definitions of assets, SMEs, and the role of infrastructure projects. Due to this confusion, PIs often make independent decisions within their own projects regarding how to leverage expertise, who qualifies as an SME, and how to engage with SMEs. This can result in wide variation across projects and may mean

[1] https://science.nasa.gov/sciact-team/arctic-earth-signs/

that SciAct is not fully leveraging NASA's suite of assets. The committee identified several questions related to leveraging NASA's assets and connecting with SMEs, which included the following:

- Are derivatives of primary NASA assets (e.g., a simplified dataset for use with middle school students that was derived from a more comprehensive NASA dataset) considered assets for the purposes of SciAct?
- Who is considered a NASA SME (e.g., can a heliophysicist at a university that uses NASA data be considered an SME for the purposes of SciAct, even if the scientist does not work directly on a NASA grant or contract; or can a graduate student fill the role of SME)?
- How are infrastructure projects for SciAct identified (i.e., why are some NASA citizen science projects considered SciAct infrastructure projects and others not?) and, as infrastructure projects, how are they supporting SciAct goals?
- What kinds of metrics are infrastructure projects reporting, and how are they assessed relative to other SciAct projects?
- How is SciAct funding used to support infrastructure projects, and are those projects effectively competing against other potential SciAct projects for this funding?

Exploring the answers to these questions within the SciAct learning community could enhance work across the portfolio in SciAct 3.0.

Refining and Expanding the Concept of Expertise

Questions related to the nature, value, and use of scientific expertise within SciAct have been recurring themes as the program has evolved. Given the multitude of ways that SciAct projects are designed to engage learners, SciAct PIs may benefit from multiple types of expertise to meet their goals. Projects bring individuals with a range of backgrounds and connections to NASA's work. In some cases, an SME might be a senior scientist working directly on a NASA mission. In other cases, an SME might be a post-doctoral fellow or graduate student connected to the mission. Some projects might engage with scientists who are not connected to NASA work but who bring deep knowledge of a relevant scientific discipline.

Many of SciAct 2.0's projects rely on a traditional model of engaging with SMEs: that is, projects often partner with an individual who possesses formal scientific knowledge, and through collaboration with SciAct project leadership, the project makes that knowledge accessible to non-expert learners. However, as SciAct projects work more closely with local communities, PIs may find that traditional notions of scientific expertise (i.e., deep experience with scientific research and professional knowledge of a science domain) are insufficient for projects that aim to connect meaningfully with learners and communities.[2] It may be important for SciAct 3.0 projects to involve experts who can help design learning experiences that leverage the considerable assets learners bring through their participation in SciAct projects.

Contemporary definitions of scientific expertise extend well beyond individual facility with scientific knowledge. Instead of settling on one specific definition of expertise, the committee posits that scientific expertise may be variable in appearance: expertise might include the ability to engage in scientific work (e.g., building and managing data repositories), or it may involve the ability to use scientific thinking to solve problems (e.g., using data to model local risks and plan for resilience). As SciAct projects increasingly partner with communities, expertise could also involve deep knowledge of a specific place, such as shared interpersonal experiences with community elders or other stakeholders who are acknowledged experts on local challenges.

Several SciAct projects emphasize shared goal setting and decision making, along with the notion of listening to communities and designing projects to address community priorities. In the community-centered approaches in SciAct 2.0, the notion of expertise is expanded beyond NASA scientists and engineers to include the knowledge and skills contributed by all project participants. This approach of honoring participants' knowledge has been demonstrated as pedagogically effective, supportive of more dimensions of individual science literacy (e.g., agency and identity), and it is an effective strategy for working across cultural differences (NASEM, 2024). Honoring participant knowledge can also advance diversity goals by expanding the modes of scientific inquiry; introducing new, egalitarian processes into science; and enlarging an artificially narrow, Western-biased history of science (Eder et al., 2023). Finally, honoring all participants' knowledge and skills can improve science by adding new lines of evidence and introducing new questions and methods (Cole et al., 2024; Gibbons & Pérez-Stable, 2024).

LEARNING ECOSYSTEMS WITHIN THE SCIENCE ACTIVATION PORTFOLIO

The 2020 National Academies assessment introduced a key idea from the learning sciences known as a "learning ecosystem" (NASEM,

[2] The committee notes that not all projects wish to engage in such partnerships, nor is it appropriate for all to do so. However, in intensive community partnerships, both NASA SMEs and knowledgeable community members can contribute to NASA's dissemination and outreach efforts.

2020, pp. 57–59). As that report noted, "STEM learning ecosystems are commonly conceptualized as the array of learning opportunities, both physical and virtual, available to members of a community." The learning ecosystem concept can help designers of learning experiences consider how learning experiences take place across settings (e.g., schools, homes, museums, science centers, faith-based institutions, libraries, camps, and online; Barron, 2006; Bevan, 2016; Ito et al., 2013; Pinkard, 2019). Various individuals and organizations participate in learning ecosystems, including peers, multi-generational family groups, facilitators, and SMEs (NASEM, 2020). Learning ecosystems are not designed in pursuit of specific learning outcomes; rather, they are understood as the broader contexts in which individual and community learning can take place.

Several SciAct 2.0 projects seek to enrich learning ecosystems to varying degrees. Specifically, they embed learning experiences in multiple locations within the community and seek to foster networked learning opportunities. One notable example is the Gulf of Maine Research Institute's (GMRI's) Learning Ecosystems Northeast (LENE) project, which explicitly focuses on collaborative communities of practice comprising a connected learning ecosystem that leverages NASA's climate data and other assets and expertise. The organizations involved work in concert with GMRI, using both virtual interactions and physical site visits to co-develop a learning ecosystem with multiple points of contact and pathways for interconnected STEM learning. Collaborators include libraries, schools, science centers, community science data teams, 4-H, and Tribal youth programs. School groups participate in field trips to collect data, SMEs work with youth in science centers to introduce relevant climate ideas, and collaborative teams build summer reading lists of related literature—together providing numerous forms of engagement for Maine youth. This is an especially compelling approach for a project that serves a disparate, heavily rural population, in that it can leverage local organizations' involvement while also helping to coordinate statewide efforts.

A similar rural project that employs an ecosystem model is the Arctic and Earth SIGNs, which operates at the University of Alaska, Fairbanks. This project taps into the expertise and priorities of Indigenous communities and supports the participation of youth in conferences where they share their research findings. This project also creates community science data-gathering activities with informal educators and using GLOBE. As with the LENE project, 4-H is an important resource that connects to local universities and rural communities, fostering linkages across regions and institutions.

Digital engagements can play an important role in learning ecosystems. The Institute for Global Environment Strategies' NASA Earth Science

Education Collaborative[3] shows clever use of online spaces and social media, including Instagram reel short-form videos and sharable media to celebrate data-collection milestones, along with virtual internships facilitated by online communications tools. As with other learning ecosystem projects, school-based experiences, informal institutions (e.g., Girl Scouts and camps), and citizen science programs are jointly working to leverage NASA assets and encourage scientific investigation.

In all, SciAct 2.0 demonstrates strategic investments in projects that seek to expand diverse learning ecosystems in ways that are responsive to community composition. These projects vary in program duration, modality, and geographic coverage. Future investments can create additional points of contact and pathways for learners who are expected to traverse multiple types of currently unconnected learning spaces.

Building a robust ecosystem requires more than simply asking sites to develop and implement individual learning experiences. Collaboration between sites is key for uncovering the specific affordances and expertise unique to each site, and for determining how learning experiences can be designed so that learners' experiences across sites are connected and meaningful. Creation of a learning ecosystem is time-intensive work. Individuals involved early in the process of establishing a SciAct-supported ecosystem may primarily focus on forging new partnerships and beginning the initial work of program creation. Established ecosystems might focus more on how resources are used across sites and how new partners might contribute. Indicators of compelling learning ecosystem projects can include the presence of multiple institutional venues or types (e.g., formal, informal, online) that strategically leverage unique assets of that venue or type of interaction.

Lastly, not all project models lend themselves to an ecosystem approach. Landmark events, such as a solar eclipse or the passing of a rare comet, are valuable opportunities for SciAct but may not be intended to produce an infrastructure that lasts beyond the duration of a specific event. However, while the committee acknowledges diminishing return on investment following a time-bound event, we also recognize the importance of balancing investment in projects driven by a major event with those with ongoing activity. Ultimately, successful learning ecosystems involve long-term investment, in the form of both consistent organization-connecting personnel and funds to address costs related to maintenance of relationships, programs, and resources. Although not all projects will use this model, the committee finds value in leveraging an ecosystems approach where appropriate.

[3] https://science.nasa.gov/sciact-team/nesec/

EXPANDING COMMUNITY-CENTERED APPROACHES

As described in Chapter 3, SciAct 2.0 has evolved to include more projects that are co-designed and co-led with communities, focus on broader community outcomes, and contribute to community scientific literacy. Many projects include communities whose members have historically been underrepresented in science and/or whose knowledge has been historically underappreciated in mainstream science: many of these projects were added to the SciAct portfolio following the call to increase the number of projects aimed at broadening participation in STEM. Specifically, the committee notes that communities engaged in this work often represent racially minoritized demographic groups, disabled communities, and Indigenous communities, among others (see Chapter 3 for SciAct 2.0's achievements in broadening participation).

Community-centered projects, as part of a spectrum of approaches, are a valuable addition to the SciAct portfolio because they are designed to directly benefit specific participants and communities, and they offer lessons that can improve NASA's engagement, especially with communities with which it has not historically engaged. Community-centered approaches are also at the cutting edge of science engagement and education research and practice; as such, they help guide the overall SciAct portfolio and enrich all component projects. Key areas of learning from community-focused parts of the SciAct portfolio include strategies for advancing diversity, equity, inclusion, and accessibility (DEIA); approaches that enhance community science literacy and agency; and an expanded understanding of expertise. This section describes how SciAct could benefit from strategically deepening its commitment to community-centered approaches, as well as further considerations for SciAct as it expands its focus in this way.

Why Expand Community-Centered Approaches?

Evaluation of SciAct 2.0 at both the project and portfolio levels suggests that community-centered approaches to science engagement contribute to many of SciAct's mid-level objectives (MLOs), namely diversity of participants (MLO 3b), identity as science learners (MLO 1a), process of science (MLO 2a), learner-centered approaches (MLO 3a), development of STEM career skills (MLO 3c), and external partnerships (MLO 4b).

A growing body of evidence indicates that community-centered processes can produce positive community outcomes, including beneficial policy, regulatory, or decision-making outcomes (Ballard et al., 2017; d'Armengol et al., 2018; Dilling & Lemos, 2011; Dosemagen & Parker, 2019; Johnson et al., 2018; Oetzel et al., 2017; Shepard, 2002; Teresa et al., 2023). For instance, community-centered work (i.e., co-production) on climate change adaptation and mitigation is well documented to increase community resilience and reduce greenhouse gas emissions (Dilling & Lemos, 2011; Johnson et al., 2018). Climate change is particularly relevant to NASA, but similar findings are documented in content areas related to public health, where the term "community-based participatory research" is used (Oetzl et al., 2017; Teresa et al., 2023). In forestry, land management, and fisheries management, the term "adaptive co-management" is frequently used to describe such research (d'Armengol et al., 2018). The environmental justice field is driven toward concrete goals, and science-based policy changes have resulted from such work (Shepard, 2002). Several co-led and co-managed citizen science projects have also produced positive community outcomes (Ballard et al., 2017; Dosemagen & Parker, 2019).

Community approaches to science are well positioned to support SciAct's DEIA goals. Best practices for science outreach and engagement with communities historically underserved by and underrepresented in science include collaborative approaches and co-creation (Bevan et al., 2020; Pandya, 2012). Collaborative and community-centered approaches can foreground research and action priorities of underserved and underrepresented communities across disciplines, including public health fields (Wallerstein et al., 2017), environmental justice (Bullard, 2007), climate justice (Djenontin & Meadow, 2018), adaptive co-management (d'Armengol et al., 2018), and science education (Cook-Sather, 2020). Many Indigenous knowledge systems center collaboration and co-creation (Yua et al., 2022).

Considerations for Community Approaches in SciAct 3.0

In the committee's discussions with project leaders and evaluators, several SciAct project leaders emphasized their projects' goals around community service, community value, and good community relationships. However, some project leaders expressed concern about the tension between NASA's dissemination goals and their projects' goals of serving communities. For example, what if community priorities are not well served by the assets, missions, or science content NASA emphasizes? By and large, however, project leaders reported success in finding overlap between community priorities and NASA assets and expertise.

Furthermore, project leaders expressed some uncertainty around NASA's overall support for community service goals. Specific concerns included the following:

- Working to support community priorities requires NASA SMEs to develop new skills and dispositions, and many SMEs have not been trained or socialized in such competencies.

- Some NASA SMEs harbor deficit-based models (i.e., based on perceived weaknesses of individuals or groups) and narrow definitions of expertise that undermine community partnerships.
- Metrics for measuring project impact currently requested by SciAct may not capture the diverse impacts of community-centered approaches, which could impact how community relationships and community-engaged work would be recognized, evaluated, and included in SciAct outcomes and impacts.
- Serving community goals requires deep, long-lasting community engagement that can extend beyond the timelines for SciAct solicitations, even though the timeline afforded in NASA grants is longer than many typical science solicitations.

Several pedagogical experts, evaluators, community leaders, and past SciAct project leads talked to the committee about their community co-leadership experiences and called for an increased use of community-centered practices across the SciAct portfolio. In SciAct 2.0, community co-leadership showed up in several ways: increased use of community advisory boards, co-management of project processes, and co-design of projects from the ground up. Community-centered projects make up almost half of the SciAct 2.0 portfolio, and community partners include both geographic communities and communities of affinity (e.g., NASA's Neurodiversity Network[4] or Eclipse Soundscapes,[5] which engage with people who are blind or low vision).

Both increased community leadership and increased centering of community priorities involve a sharing of power, decision making, and leadership between science- or education-based experts and community members and leaders with their own expertise. Some SciAct 2.0 project leaders described themselves as facilitators, intermediaries, and boundary spanners. In this role, they

- Actively search for and pursue areas in which community priorities and NASA assets overlap;
- Develop strategies to promote shared power and decision making;
- Assist NASA SMEs to equitably collaborate with communities and recognize and value community expertise;
- Work with community leaders and community members to encourage and support co-leadership and "elevate community voice;" and
- Work with the entire project team to connect knowledge to concrete community outcomes.

---

[4] https://science.nasa.gov/sciact-team/nasa-neurodiversity-network/
[5] https://science.nasa.gov/sciact-team/eclipse-soundscapes/

Deepening SciAct's commitment to community approaches does not mean that all projects in the portfolio are expected to adopt this approach. Indeed, both NASA and SciAct have clearly identified educational and dissemination priorities that are well served by the science-centered approaches identified in Chapter 3. Rather, the committee observes that the SciAct 3.0 portfolio could better reflect, support, and share outcomes from the growing cadre of projects that are more community centered, thus supporting robust outcomes in the areas described earlier in this chapter.

MEETING THE UNIQUE NEEDS OF SPECIFIC PROJECTS

As described in Chapter 3, the SciAct 2.0 portfolio varies across several dimensions—geography, discipline, formal or informal settings, age groups, and partners. SciAct 2.0 projects vary by depth/breadth of engagement and nature of the engagement strategy (i.e., along a continuum from dissemination driven to fully community centered). This diversity helps SciAct address its MLOs, offers learning opportunities that leverage multiple methodologies and modalities, and potentially creates a diverse STEM learning ecosystem.

Realizing this potential, however, requires attention to the unique needs of specific project types, strategies for coordinating work across projects and promoting cross-project learning, and a transparent vision of overall SciAct success that helps projects understand their potential contributions to that vision. This section focuses on meeting the unique needs of specific project types.

Project Timelines and Deliverables

Some needs are shared by most, if not all, SciAct projects, whether they focus on deep co-creation with small community groups or broad science dissemination. These needs include

- Knowledge of effective science communication strategies;
- Ability to find, adapt, and leverage NASA assets (including but not limited to SMEs);
- Grounding in sophisticated, up-to-date understanding of the learning sciences and education research; and
- Pragmatic, actionable, and evidence-based practices for advancing DEIA, even in hostile political landscapes.

SciAct can benefit from continuing to support these important, foundational needs through its learning community approach and its technical and social infrastructure.

The spectrum of modes of engagement also has implications for supporting project timelines and deliverables. Proposals, including those to SciAct, often ask for clearly articulated projects goals, outcomes, strategies, and evaluation plans. Although these requirements are important considerations for all PIs, they have particular consequences for partnered projects, which rely on relationship building to negotiate working agreements and which engage in collaborative determination of project goals, outcomes, and strategies. Such foundation-setting collaboration necessitates significant work for both PIs and communities, which often occurs without financial support. Projects that work with partners (community-engaged approaches in particular) often foster relationships over timeframes that extend beyond a single funding cycle. Additionally, project staff may be challenged to navigate differing expectations around time and labor: that is, working with communities may involve designing programming that does not neatly fit within the bounds of a semester-based timeframe or government contract, and deadlines and priorities may shift as the needs of communities evolve over time. Bridging the gap between subject matter content and learners' needs and expectations often requires time, patience, and knowledge sharing, much of which relies on relationships across parties (Soleri et al., 2016).

It may be important for projects that leverage partnerships to pivot or pause due to external factors or changes in outside priorities. For instance, testimony from project staff described a project in which recovery from a natural disaster impacted a community's capacity for and prioritization of work on curriculum co-development. Project teams need capacity, at minimum, to pause work in such cases; even better would be the ability to pivot toward the emergent community priority. For example, instead of continuing to center a SciAct project on curriculum, the project could pivot toward leveraging NASA assets to support recovery. For these reasons, an increase in community-engagement approaches within the SciAct 3.0 portfolio may require even more flexibility and adaptability in project timelines and funding mechanisms.

Lastly, partnership building with communities takes time: relationships are built over multiple interactions and require ongoing attention and care. For community-engaged projects, significant work and investment is often asked of community partners, some of which may occur outside of the bounds of a government contract or academic timeframe, as noted above. In determining whether a project is well positioned for success, SciAct may want to consider whether the project has demonstrated sufficient evidence of an emerging partnership and whether the project has included sufficient time to deepen that partnership in support of shared learning goals. Concurrently, SciAct could find value in examining how its operational structures (e.g., expectations around timing, compensation processes) either facilitate or constrain projects' engagement with community partners. Analyzing operational structures and sharing best practices across projects could facilitate equitable support of communities and community-based organizations.

Evaluation and Impact

All projects in the SciAct portfolio need tools to communicate their impact in ways that speak to overall SciAct goals while remaining authentic to the project's learning goals, modes of engagement, and choices about scope and breadth. Some project PIs reported that portfolio-level metrics require extra work and add little value to their projects or, at worst, that tools provided for portfolio-level evaluation are inconsistent with project-level learning goals or modes of engagement.

As described in Chapter 3, a large event might focus on sparking interest across a broad group of participants, while a more community-engaged project may focus on supporting identity development and science agency among a smaller group of people. PIs of projects characterized by more intense engagement with fewer participants noted that the overall metrics collected across the portfolio did not allow them to adequately communicate the value of their projects. As one PI noted, "How is my little program with 10 teachers going to look when compared to an event that reaches 10,000?" More metrics appropriate for projects that deeply engage a small number of people and better tools for characterizing the "ripple" or downstream impacts from those projects could be helpful.

Furthermore, projects that center community engagement could more readily demonstrate their impact with more robust reporting metrics. Many such projects have designed project-level evaluations, often in collaboration with community members, that marry science, education, research, and community goals—these complex project evaluations are challenging to translate into current SciAct portfolio-level metrics.

Updating the Theory of Action

SciAct project staff reported to the committee that they would like to see SciAct leadership refine SciAct's existing "theory of action" to better include the work of community-centered projects. Community-centered projects give extra attention to community engagement, long-term relationship building, co-creation, and knowledge mobilization. Such projects attempt to respectfully weave together disparate ways of knowing by joining NASA's scientific expertise with community expertise, and they center community learning, agency, and identity. For many community-centered projects (e.g., GMRI's LENE or Native Earth | Native Sky), individual project evaluations capture project outcomes. Evaluators who focused on these projects, however, noted that SciAct's current MLOs are not structured to capture successes that emanate from community approaches. Project leads and evaluators also suggested that a next step in portfolio-level infrastructure might focus on efforts to capture and share learnings and outcomes that result from community-centered work.

In general, it seems the current theory of action across the SciAct portfolio is better aligned with and well suited for the dissemination-driven approaches described in Chapter 3. As a result, SciAct may well be accomplishing more than it is measuring. A comprehensive theory of action across the portfolio could better represent the many kinds of science activation outcomes, help align metrics toward those outcomes, and help balance the portfolio of projects to achieve this expanded set of outcomes. Furthermore, a more comprehensive theory of action could help clarify how these emergent community-centered approaches complement traditional approaches in supporting SciAct's overall success, as well as help identify opportunities for links across approaches—either in terms of knowledge sharing for project leads or building cross-project pathways for learners.

It is important for any theory of action to continue to welcome and celebrate goals and projects that have long characterized SciAct. Content-driven and event-driven projects continue to play important roles in the portfolio and are uniquely situated to contribute to MLOs. For instance, the Sea Level Education, Awareness, and Literacy project focuses on producing actionable information on sea-level rise and making it available to decision makers in coastal regions. A comprehensive theory of action could help to situate these activities as part of a spectrum of engagement and learning approaches, as well as allow a meta-analysis of the alignment of specific approaches with specific outcomes.

THE POTENTIAL OF PROFESSIONAL LEARNING IN SCIENCE ACTIVATION

One way that SciAct could amplify its impact is by improving its ability to learn within its own professional learning community. Although SciAct has made tremendous strides in creating an infrastructure to support a coordinated network of projects (as described in Chapter 3), further efforts to strengthen the work of the network, improve ongoing communication, and facilitate collaboration across projects could benefit SciAct 3.0. In this section, we offer insight into practices of successful professional learning communities and consider future implications for SciAct.

Enhancing the SciAct Professional Learning Community

In the committee's opinion, SciAct has the potential to develop its existing network structures into a professional learning community, in which individual project teams can better build and share knowledge across the SciAct portfolio. This could be viewed as the SciAct portfolio hosting a professional community of practice. The concept of communities of practice comes from research on learning in situ across settings, including through professional organizations, informal networks, and interpersonal relationships (Brown & Duguid, 1991; Lave & Wenger, 1991; Wenger, 1998).

Communities of practice complement the idea of a learning ecosystem, which emphasizes the presence of multiple organizations and resources in a professional learning community. While these terms have been used interchangeably, the distinctions across terms are important for SciAct: we use the term learning ecosystem to describe the constellation of organizations and spaces that comprise the context for community and individual learning. Professional learning communities refer to the networks or shared reflective spaces created to facilitate learning and growth in professional settings, comprised of professional organizations or other community entities. Communities of practice, however, create similar learning opportunities but are entirely comprised of individual practitioners. Professional learning communities have additional features stemming from the communities of practice literature, which is heavily employed in learning sciences and organizational learning research. Drawing upon a synthesis by Hoadley (2012), key features of a professional learning community include the following:

- *Authentic practices.* Core practices of professional learning communities are authentic to that community, meaning that they are practices of "experts." For instance, all SciAct projects may publicize their events, prepare staff or intermediaries for public engagement, negotiate permissions, or select relevant NASA assets. These are important practices that, in combination, are specific to SciAct projects and are core foci for learning within the community of practice.
- *Variable degrees of experience and expertise.* Professional learning communities include people with differing levels of experience along with unique and complementary expertise. For example, veteran practitioners are commonly assumed to be highly experienced, with greater expertise in the practices of a community than "newcomers." However, time spent in the community or engaging in an aspect of the practice does not necessarily reflect one's capacity to play the role of an "old-timer." Rather, old-timers typically represent some of the most advanced and highly valued ways of engaging in the practices of a community.

- *Changing trajectories in participation.* Learning in professional learning communities involves shifts in participation in community practices. For example, in legitimate peripheral participation, newcomers first participate in activities that may appear more ancillary to the central practices, but by doing so they observe or otherwise gain exposure to the central practice. For instance, in a carpentry shop, a new apprentice may begin by ordering supplies, sharpening tools, and maintaining the woodshop—tasks that expose the apprentice to the range of "higher" tasks in master carpentry, in which they will eventually participate.
- *Connections between practitioners.* Connections between participants in a professional learning community are mandatory and can occur through both synchronous and asynchronous means, and through in-person and digital interactions.
- *Information retention.* While interactions between experienced and novice practitioners are important for learning, methods of knowledge retention—such as written cases, recorded tips and cautions for similar projects, or pre-curated asset collections for specific tasks—are important resources to build and utilize. It is also important that these are not built just for the sake of creating a repository or creating records. Methods of knowledge are most beneficial when they are considered useful and usable by community members and practitioners.
- *Awareness of community resources.* Beyond artifacts that support information retention, another community resource consists of community members with useful knowledge or expertise. Learning communities can capitalize on these resources by establishing mechanisms to spread, maintain, and update awareness of available resources.
- *Multiple mechanisms of addressing problems of practice.* For some community learning needs, simply hearing or sharing information or resources can be adequate. However, learning can be supported and problems of practice solved by other documented methods. For example, novel problems can be identified and jointly solved between practitioners. The opportunity for multiple forms of interaction can enable multiple learning mechanisms to operate within a community.

Additionally, key learning subcommunities (e.g., role-specific communities of practitioners, communities of like organizations, communities of practitioners serving similar demographic communities) can exist within a larger professional learning community. These subcommunities can have shared problems of practice to address or otherwise have a strong affinity for one another. For instance, in SciAct, multiple groups may host museum events and thus comprise a sensible subcommunity that can address key problems and solutions to increasing engagement with science and NASA assets. Community science groups may similarly benefit from forming a subcommunity.

Creating time and space for knowledge sharing and professional learning community development could involve an intense inventory of the various goals that projects are pursuing, where and how project team members gain professional knowledge relevant to development and implementation of SciAct programs, and how NASA could provide infrastructure to support multiple points of contact with valuable knowledge. For example, such efforts might include

- Creation of online communities through asynchronous communications systems;
- SciAct newsletters that profile specific design processes;
- Public guide documents that synthesize common challenges or techniques across projects to help onboard new projects or share with existing ones; and
- Convenings at which new findings from within the SciAct community about the design of effective programs are explicitly foregrounded.

To inject new knowledge from outside sources, learning experts from other fields who have undertaken similar types of work and thus have research insights and recommendations could be invited guests at convenings. SciAct may also begin asking for strategies and frameworks as official project outputs, to encourage the generation of such knowledge. Based on work in other fields focused on designing learning experiences, several nuances are relevant. For example, projects working with classroom teachers have different concerns and strategies for effectiveness than do projects working with public science communication, which also differ from projects working with informal science learning organizations.

With appropriate attention to knowledge production and sharing, SciAct's efforts could contribute to a larger professional learning ecosystem that would transcend the work of individual projects and help inform NASA on how to better support education and engagement. Such an endeavor will take time and thus a roadmap for its creation, including adequate time for establishment and appropriate indicators of effectiveness, would be appropriate.

Roles of SciAct Leadership and Infrastructure to Support Projects

SciAct's existing activities and structures suggest that multiple opportunities for information exchange and sharing of lessons exist across projects. Some arrangements are formalized in cross-collaboration agreements, while others arise as a result of opportunities for engagement across projects. Examples include the following:

- The annual SciAct meeting, structured to provide opportunities for identifying and building collaborations. For example, the schedule of the 2023 meeting included topic-centered breakout sessions (including Science Misson Directorate [SMD] division topics), strategies to engage participants and establish partnerships, and sessions for special interest groups (e.g., broadening participation, data literacy and open science, diversability, rural areas, digital learning, American Indian/Alaska Native, women/girls, visualization). Each morning included a showcase session in which individual projects were presented at exhibit tables to promote cross-project learning and communication.
- The Learning Ecosystem Meeting, held in 2023 in Arizona. This meeting included concurrent sessions organized around project topics, strategies for engagement, and cultivation of partnerships with communities historically underserved by and underrepresented in science.
- Regular monthly meetings, including those held to convene PIs and local project evaluators, and one-on-one project meetings with SciAct leadership.
- Collaborations formed by a subset of projects for the regular exchange of ideas.
- A SciAct-sponsored shared communication platform and shared Google drive as a central information-sharing hub.

For many project teams, particularly those established in SciAct 1.0, the SciAct community is an excellent source of ideas, collaborators, learning, and connections to NASA assets and expertise. However, committee discussions with some SciAct project leadership, particularly those from projects recently added to the SciAct portfolio, found that SciAct does not appear to provide sufficient support or necessary infrastructure for project staff to truly utilize these resources. Ongoing support for cross-project learning could further amplify meaningful collaboration across projects, learning from other projects' successes and challenges, and identification of project-appropriate SMEs or scientific assets. For example, some PIs stated that monthly meetings were too heavily focused on sharing quad charts that were not meaningful for many projects, and that the two-hour timeframe was too long to stay engaged. SciAct's annual meeting was consistently cited as a valuable experience, in that collaboration, sharing, and camaraderie were encouraged. Based on discussions with PIs and project teams, there is an opportunity to continue evolving the annual meeting to allow more time for ideation, innovation, deeper discussions around topics of shared interest, as well as discussion of NASA assets and new research potentially relevant to SciAct projects.

The committee commends SciAct's leadership team for the significant changes instituted over the past five years. SciAct leadership has made efforts toward implementing all recommendations noted in the 2020 National Academies assessment. With respect to the SciAct leadership team overall, an opportunity exists for designated staff to engage more fully with SciAct projects. For example, one PI suggested selecting SciAct staff members who are responsible for diving deeply into a group of projects within the same SMD discipline (e.g., Earth science, heliophysics) or projects that share an intended audience (e.g., informal science educators, middle school teachers), so that the staff member could suggest effective collaborations among projects; introduce PIs to appropriate NASA assets or SMEs; and recommend content reviewers, guest scientists, and other stakeholders with relevant expertise. Such additional support could further the collective impact approach and ensure that all projects can access the best partners, scientific assets, and expertise to succeed and, in turn, increase SciAct's overall impact.

SUMMARY

Building on the success of SciAct 2.0, the committee highlighted five areas in which SciAct could broaden its reach and deepen its impact in SciAct 3.0: strengthening how expertise is recognized and utilized throughout the portfolio, considering how learning ecosystems are supported and leveraged within SciAct, improving and expanding community-centered approaches in funded projects, meeting the unique needs of specific projects, and improving SciAct's ability to learn in its own professional learning community. The following conclusions summarize the committee's considerations for where SciAct 3.0 might focus its efforts.

> *Conclusion 7: The current SciAct portfolio has evolved to include projects that involve community partners and are focused on community outcomes. Accordingly, the concept of NASA assets has expanded to include both NASA assets and community assets; all assets are important to project success, but NASA assets are particularly relevant for maintaining connections to NASA's work and SciAct's mission.*

Conclusion 8: SciAct has not provided a clear and consistent definition of subject matter experts. As a result, SciAct project leaders cannot be sure whether the expertise leveraged in their projects can be considered a NASA asset.

Conclusion 9: Co-design and collaboration with communities is an emerging strategy across several SciAct projects. These approaches are supportive of SciAct's larger goals related to diversity, equity, inclusion, and accessibility.

Conclusion 10: The number of NASA infrastructure projects has increased over time, in the absence of a deliberate strategy describing how these projects fit within the larger SciAct portfolio or how they are intended to support it.

5

Recommendations for SciAct 3.0

In the wake of this second assessment of National Aeronautics and Space Administration's (NASA's) Science Activation program (SciAct), the National Academies of Sciences, Engineering, and Medicine's (National Academies') Committee to Assess NASA Science Activation 2.0 has identified a suite of recommendations that, if implemented, can further propel SciAct toward meeting its goals. SciAct has made considerable progress since the first National Academies assessment (NASEM, 2020): not only has SciAct acted upon every recommendation outlined in the first report, but the program has also taken additional steps to support the projects in its portfolio. Building on these accomplishments, this chapter reiterates opportunities for improvement observed across the current assessment. These observations are intended as probes for SciAct as it plans its 3.0 programming: the committee offers these ideas in the spirit of helping SciAct sharpen its focus and expand upon its initial efforts. Formal recommendations, intended to capitalize on SciAct's ongoing work, are provided at the end of the chapter.

OPPORTUNITIES FOR IMPROVEMENT: INTENTIONAL COMMUNICATION

This report identified several areas in which SciAct leadership could strengthen the program through intentional decision making, clearly communicated to the entire SciAct portfolio. Various examples illustrate instances in which intentional decisions could support programmatic success. First, although the 2020 National Academies assessment delineated an operational theory of change, SciAct principal investigators (PIs) and project staff repeatedly identified the need for further guidance outlining how leadership's expectations of SciAct projects will serve the portfolio's objectives. As discussed in Chapter 2, the logic model developed by SciAct's portfolio-level evaluators (Pacific Research and Evaluation [PRE]) does not clearly identify specific outcomes or outputs, nor does it reflect how SciAct expects its program and project inputs and activities to lead to desired outcomes.

The committee noted additional decision-making opportunities for SciAct leadership, through which decisions could inform the actions and directions of others—that is, by making an intentional decision in each of these realms, other actors in the portfolio will be enabled to pursue their own programmatic work more effectively. We offer the following provocations:

- What types of equity-related goals or outcomes does SciAct hope to effect?
- What balance does SciAct wish to strike across dissemination-driven and community-centered approaches to programming?
- What does "success" look like in terms of connecting with Science Mission Directorate (SMD) assets?
- What types of portfolio-level success would SciAct like to demonstrate/communicate to outside stakeholders?

COMMUNICATING SCIENCE ACTIVATION IMPACTS AND RELEVANCE ACROSS NASA AND BEYOND

The SciAct portfolio clearly contributes to NASA's strategic goals and objectives, particularly Strategic Objective 4.3: build the next generation of explorers (NASA, 2022). Sharing data, information, and knowledge with the public is very much part of NASA's vision and responsibility as a federal agency. SciAct is analogous to other programs within SMD, as it has its own goals, objectives, and program-specific requirements. There is an opportunity for SciAct to explicitly connect its objectives, successes, and impacts to NASA's strategic priorities and decadal plans in ways that inform NASA, particularly on community-centered practices. The decadal plans released to date indicate significant challenges in building and sustaining a diverse pipeline of professionals. SciAct could help NASA engage with communities historically underserved by and underrepresented in science, thereby building interest in and excitement about STEM careers within those communities.

SciAct has clearly made efforts to share its learnings beyond NASA, including with the broader education community. Several projects have published their experiences and learnings in education research outlets, and presentations highlighting SciAct projects are common at professional society annual meetings. Given the unique design of SciAct within the federal landscape, there is an opportunity to learn from the program's ongoing work as a professional learning community: What has SciAct learned that could benefit other programs? Where and how has SciAct succeeded in supporting learning across the portfolio? Documenting these observations could benefit the larger education landscape, and SciAct leadership may want to consider how to best communicate these successes to NASA and beyond.

FINAL THOUGHTS AND RECOMMENDATIONS

The committee commends SciAct leadership for the progress achieved over the past five years in addressing the recommendations put forth in the 2020 National Academies assessment. The SciAct portfolio clearly contributes to NASA's strategic goals and objectives in meaningful ways. SciAct has the opportunity to explicitly connect its goals, objectives, and successes/impacts to NASA's strategic priorities and decadal plans in ways that inform NASA, particularly on community-centered practices. The unique design of SciAct within the federal landscape provides an opportunity to learn from SciAct's ongoing work as a professional learning community, and for sharing its successes within NASA and beyond. Designated SciAct staff could lead the coordination of such efforts.

To complement SciAct's decision making in the above areas, we offer several formal recommendations for immediate action. We believe that these recommendations will bring SciAct even closer to meeting its stated objectives.

Recommendation 1: SciAct should be transparent about the goals of its portfolio evaluation and clear about its intentions for using evaluation results. Furthermore, in light of the portfolio's diverse nature, the evaluation should consider measuring SciAct's impact through multiple measures instead of a single measure. To capture the breadth and depth of project work, the portfolio-level evaluation should utilize methods that highlight stories and narratives of learning and change.

As articulated in Chapter 3, the decision to hire a portfolio-level evaluator is a direct response to a recommendation outlined in the 2020 National Academies assessment. PRE made efforts to provide portfolio-level feedback, but the current committee recognizes that SciAct's diverse portfolio may not be well served by the use of single, quantitative measures of programmatic success. The 2020 National Academies assessment outlined a series of potential goals for a portfolio-level evaluation, including

- Deepening understanding of how individual projects align with SciAct goals;
- Improving portfolio-level coherence throughout all stages of project planning, implementation, and assessment;
- Surfacing unique and promising trends within the portfolio;
- Identifying areas for improvement on a continual basis;
- Representing one mechanism for feedback between SciAct network members and SciAct leadership;
- Developing potential models for understanding SciAct's impact; and
- Directly facilitating participation routines across the network that support participatory knowledge building, problem and goal identification, and impact assessment approaches (NASEM, 2020, p. 86).

While the PRE evaluation considered many of these potential goals, SciAct could benefit from clarity and transparency around the specific goals the portfolio-level evaluation is pursuing as well as how SciAct intends to use the evaluation's findings. It is important for SciAct project staff and evaluators to understand how they are expected to respond to the portfolio-level evaluation, as well as to feel confident that their successes and challenges will be reflected in evaluation efforts. To achieve this goal, the portfolio-level evaluation may consider expanding its scope to capture the portfolio's diversity of approaches to supporting STEM learning and engagement and aggregate project contributions across a range of axes rather than a single measure.

Recommendation 2: In building the next iteration of its portfolio, SciAct should consider further investment in community-centered approaches to programming. In expanding this investment, SciAct should ensure that future funded projects attend to modes of engagement and learning that center community-engaged approaches.

The committee was impressed by SciAct's success in deepening its commitment to broadening participation in STEM through the addition of a suite of new projects in SciAct 2.0. Since the 2020 National Academies assessment, the value of approaching educational opportunities from a community-centered lens has been increasingly appreciated throughout the education research landscape. As described in Chapter 4, community-centered approaches to STEM engagement overlap considerably with SciAct's programmatic objectives. Thus, it is important for SciAct to intentionally seek out new projects with community-centered approaches, with the overall goal of expanding the portfolio's capacity in this area.

Recommendation 3: As SciAct continues its commitment to broadening participation, it should develop strategies for engaging with audiences and communities that have been historically excluded from NASA and science generally, and place priority on (1) supporting existing projects that include those groups and (2) expanding the number of projects that work with those populations.

SciAct has made significant progress in expanding the diversity of groups engaged in its work. These efforts could be further strengthened by intentionally empowering and collaborating with audiences and communities that have typically been excluded by traditional scientific endeavors. To engage in this work, it will be important for SciAct to pay careful attention to *how* projects are engaging with their audiences: it is not enough to merely invite audiences into traditional science experiences—supporting participants' identities in science encompasses rethinking the involvement of audiences in project work from the outset. For example, whose questions are answered through participation in a SciAct project? Who dictates the pace of the work? For projects in the current portfolio, how can existing relationships be augmented to deepen participants' experiences? By developing a suite of programmatic strategies aligned to SciAct's equity goals, SciAct could be better positioned to meet its primary objectives.

Recommendation 4: SciAct should refine its logic model to reflect the theoretical underpinnings and theories of change by which program and project inputs and activities are expected to lead to desired outcomes, particularly with respect to community-centered approaches in which communities may set priorities and outcomes.

SciAct leadership has an opportunity to more clearly articulate its logic model so that all actors in the portfolio understand exactly how their work is intended to lead to desired outcomes. Specific refining can reflect the ways in which SciAct's expanding commitment to community-centered approaches is intended to serve the portfolio's goals, particularly when communities may see conflict between their own goals and NASA's goals. It is important for a SciAct logic model to carefully capture programmatic inputs, actions, outputs, and outcomes such that all projects can see the relationship between meeting their own goals and meeting the portfolio's mid-level and top-level objectives. In expressly articulating this logic model, SciAct can attend to the richness afforded by the range and variety of portfolio approaches to supporting learning.

Recommendation 5: Given the importance of leveraging NASA assets for meeting the goals of SciAct, SciAct should clarify its definition of subject matter expertise. Specifically, while all projects require subject matter expertise, only some projects will leverage NASA subject matter experts (SMEs) as an identified NASA asset. SciAct should specify what is meant by SMEs and use that definition when building a portfolio that balances multiple types of asset use.

As discussed in Chapter 4, considerable confusion was noted across the portfolio around the definition of the term "subject matter expert" (SME). Given the multiple types of expertise necessary for the diversity of SciAct projects, it is important for SciAct to clarify the kinds of expertise projects require in their implementation. NASA SMEs will be an appropriate NASA asset for some projects but not all. It is important for projects to understand what "counts" as a NASA SME, so they can identify whether the expert they are using is considered a NASA asset. The SciAct portfolio will naturally make use of a range of NASA assets across projects.

Recommendation 6: SciAct should continue to build on the network structures that have been created, and develop those structures in a professional learning community, such that separate project teams can better generate and share knowledge across projects in the SciAct portfolio.

The committee was impressed by SciAct's commitment to building out a cross-project network structure, and we suggest that SciAct continue that investment. As noted in Chapter 5, SciAct can pursue multiple strategies toward even deeper success in this area, including more coordinated learning opportunities at annual and monthly PI meetings, devoted staff time for supporting network priorities, and new mechanisms for knowledge sharing. Such forms of investment could leverage the portfolio's considerable strengths toward supporting even stronger project implementation.

As part of building on these network structures, several important questions emerge for SciAct's consideration. First, given the limited capacities of SciAct PIs and project staff, the committee recognizes the importance of incentivizing participation in professional learning communities so that individual investment of time is both valued and valuable. Furthermore, given that SciAct is committed to a vision of STEM learning that reflects the most current research and practice in the field, we recognize the importance of onboarding new practitioners into these contemporary frameworks and approaches. Future iterations of SciAct may benefit from intentional opportunities to support initial baseline learning for new PIs and project staff.

This report represents the committee's attempt to harness SciAct's considerable efforts to improve the performance of its portfolio. Based on our understanding of the evidence, we believe that with additional intentional decision making around operational strategy, SciAct can more effectively pursue its top- and mid-level objectives. We remain deeply optimistic about SciAct's role in supporting STEM engagement for learners across the country, and we are honored to support SciAct as it continues to meet the nation's STEM education needs.

References

Association of Science and Technology Centers. (2024). *Approaches to community science.* https://communityscience.astc.org/approaches-to-community-science/

Balazs, C. L., & Morello-Frosch, R. (2013). The three R's: How community based participatory research strengthens the rigor, relevance, and reach of science. *Environmental Justice, 6*(1), 9–16. https://doi.org/10.1089/env.2012.0017

Ballard, H. L., Robinson, L. D., Young, A. N., Pauly, G. B., Higgins, L. M., Johnson, R. F., & Tweddle, J. C. (2017). Contributions to conservation outcomes by natural history museum-led citizen science: Examining evidence and next steps. *Biological Conservation, 208*, 87–97. https://doi.org/10.1016/j.biocon.2016.08.040

Barron, B. (2006). Interest and self-sustained learning as catalysts of development: A learning ecology perspective. *Human Development, 49*(4), 193–224. https://doi.org/10.1159/000094368

Berhe, A. A. (2023). *Federal science funding agencies play important role in broadening participation in STEM.* U.S. Department of Energy Office of Science. https://www.energy.gov/science/articles/federal-science-funding-agencies-play-important-role-broadening-participation-stem

Bevan, B. (2016). STEM learning ecologies: Relevant, responsive, and connected. *Connected Science Learning, 1*(1). https://doi.org/10.1080/24758779.2016.12420446

Bevan, B., Calabrese Barton, A., & Garibay, C. (2020). Broadening perspectives on broadening participation: Professional learning tools for more expansive and equitable science communication. *Frontiers in Communication, 5*, 52. https://doi.org/10.3389/fcomm.2020.00052

Bevc, C., Young, D., & Peterman, K. (2016). Using social network analysis to document science festival partnerships. *Journal of Science Communication, 15*(5), A04. https://doi.org/10.22323/2.15050204

Bonney, R. (2021). Expanding the impact of citizen science. *BioScience, 71*(5), 448–451. https://doi.org/10.1093/biosci/biab041

Boyette, T., & Ramsey, J. R. (2019). Does the messenger matter? Studying the impacts of scientists and engineers interacting with public audiences at science festival events. *Journal of Science Communication, 18*(2), A02. https://doi.org/10.22323/2.18020202

Brenninkmeijer, J. (2022). Achieving societal and academic impacts of research: A comparison of networks, values, and strategies. *Science and Public Policy, 49*(5), 728–738. https://doi.org/10.1093/scipol/scac022

Brown, J. S., & Duguid, P. (1991). Organizational learning and communities-of-practice: Toward a unified view of working, learning, and innovation. *Organization Science, 2*(1), 40–57. https://doi.org/10.1287/orsc.2.1.40

Bullard, R. D. (2007). Equity, unnatural man-made disasters, and race: Why environmental justice matters. In R. C. Wilkinson & W. R. Freudenburg (Eds.), *Equity and the environment* (pp. 51–85). Emerald Group Publishing Limited. https://doi.org/10.1016/S0196-1152(07)15002-X

Canovan, C. (2019). "Going to these events truly opens your eyes." Perceptions of science and science careers following a family visit to a science festival. *Journal of Science Communication, 18*(02). https://doi.org/10.22323/2.18020201

Chen, Y. C., Benus, M. J., & Hernandez, J. (2019). Managing uncertainty in scientific argumentation. *Science Education, 103*(5), 1235–1276. https://doi.org/10.1002/sce.21527

Cole, N., Kormann, E., Klebel, T., Apartis, S., & Ross-Hellauer, T. (2024). The societal impact of open science: A scoping review. *Royal Society Open Science, 11*(6), 11240286. http://doi.org/10.1098/rsos.240286

Cook-Sather, A. (2020). Respecting voices: How the co-creation of teaching and learning can support academic staff, underrepresented students, and equitable practices. *Higher Education, 79*(5), 885–901. https://doi.org/10.1007/s10734-019-00445-w

Cooper, C. B., Hawn, C. L., Larson, L. R., Parrish, J. K., Bowser, G., Cavalier, D., Dunn, R. R., Haklay, M., Kar Gupta, K., Osborne Jelks, N., Johnson, V. A., Katti, M., Leggett, Z., Wilson, O. R., & Wilson, S. (2021). Inclusion in citizen science: The conundrum of rebranding. *Science, 372*(6549), 1386–1388. https://doi.org/10.1126/science.abi6487

d'Armengol, L., Castillo, M. P., Ruiz-Mallén, I., & Corbera, E. (2018). A systematic review of co-managed small-scale fisheries: Social diversity and adaptive management improve outcomes. *Global Environmental Change, 52*, 212–225. https://doi.org/10.1016/j.gloenvcha.2018.07.009

Dilling, L., & Lemos, M. C. (2011). Creating usable science: Opportunities and constraints for climate knowledge use and their implications for science policy. *Global Environmental Change, 21*(2), 680–689. https://doi.org/10.1016/j.gloenvcha.2010.11.006

Djenontin, I. N. S., & Meadow, A. M. (2018). The art of co-production of knowledge in environmental sciences and management: Lessons from international practice. *Environmental Management, 61*(6), 885–903. https://doi.org/10.1007/s00267-018-1028-3

Dosemagen, S., & Parker, A. J. (2019). Citizen science across a spectrum: Broadening the impact of citizen science and community science. *Science & Technology Studies, 32*(2). https://doi.org/10.23987/sts.60419

Eder, M. M., D'Alonzo, K. T., Yonas, M. A., & Oetzel, J. G. (2023). Editorial: Examining community-engaged and participatory research programs and projects. *Frontiers in Public Health, 11*, 1239670. https://doi.org/10.3389/fpubh.2023.1239670

Falk, J. H., & Needham, M. D. (2011). Measuring the impact of a science center on its community. *Journal of Research in Science Teaching, 48*(1), 1–12. https://doi.org/10.1002/tea.20394

Finger, L., van den Bogaert, V., Schmidt, L., Fleischer, J., Stadtler, M., Sommer, K., & Wirth, J. (2023). The science of citizen science: A systematic literature review on educational and scientific outcomes. *Frontiers in Education, 8*. https://doi.org/10.3389/feduc.2023.1226529

Finnerty, S., Piazza, J., & Levine, M. (2024). Between two worlds: The scientist's dilemma in climate activism. *npj Climate Action, 3*(77). https://doi.org/10.1038/s44168-024-00161-x

Fischhoff, B., & Davis, A. L. (2014). Communicating scientific uncertainty. *Proceedings of the National Academy of Sciences, 111*(Suppl 4), 13664–13671.

Gibbons, G., & Pérez-Stable, E. (2024). Harnessing the power of community-engaged research *American Journal of Public Health, 114*(S7–S11). https://doi.org/10.2105/AJPH.2023.307528

Hand, V., & Gresalfi, M. (2015). The joint accomplishment of identity. *Educational Psychologist, 50*(3), 190–203. https://doi.org/10.1080/00461520.2015.1075401

Hoadley, C. (2012). What is a community of practice and how can we support it? In S. Land & D. Jonassen (Eds.), *Theoretical foundations of learning environments* (pp. 286–299). Routledge. https://doi.org/10.4324/9780203813799

Hussim, H., Rosli, R., Nor, N., Maat, S., Mahmud, M. S., Iksan, Z., Rambely, A., Mahmud, S., Halim, L., Osman, K., & Lay, A. (2024). A systematic literature review of informal STEM learning. *European Journal of STEM Education, 9*(07). https://doi.org/10.20897/ejsteme/14609

Illingworth, S. M., Lewis, E., & Percival, C. (2015). Does attending a large science event enthuse young people about science careers? *Journal of Science Communication, 14*. https://doi.org/10.22323/2.14020206

Ito, M., Gutierrez, K., Livingstone, S., Penuel, B., Rhodes, J., Salen, K., Schor, J., Sefton-Green, J., & Watkins, S. C. (2013). *Connected learning: An agenda for research and design.* Digital Media and Learning Research Hub.

Jensen, E., & Buckley, N. (2014). Why people attend science festivals: Interests, motivations and self-reported benefits of public engagement with research. *Public Understanding of Science, 23*(5), 557–573. https://doi.org/10.1177/0963662512458624

Johnson, K., Feurt, C., & Paolisso, M. (2018). Collaborative science and learning as tools for climate change adaptation planning. *The International Journal of Climate Change: Impacts and Responses, 10*(1), 59–75. https://doi.org/10.18848/1835-7156/CGP/v10i01/59-75

Kato-Nitta, N., Maeda, T., Iwahashi, K., & Tachikawa, M. (2018). Understanding the public, the visitors, and the participants in science communication activities. *Public Understanding of Science, 27*(7), 857–875. https://doi.org/10.1177/0963662517723258

Kennedy, E. B., Jensen, E. A., & Verbeke, M. (2018). Preaching to the scientifically converted: Evaluating inclusivity in science festival audiences. *International Journal of Science Education, Part B, 8*(1), 14–21. https://doi.org/10.1080/21548455.2017.1371356

Kim, A. Y., & Sinatra, G. M. (2018). Science identity development: An interactionist approach. *International Journal of STEM Education, 5*, 1–6. https://doi.org/10.1186/s40594-018-0149-9

Lave, J., & Wenger, E. (1991). *Situated learning: Legitimate peripheral participation.* Cambridge University Press.

Martin, V. Y. (2017). Citizen science as a means for increasing public engagement in science: Presumption or possibility? *Science Communication, 39*(2), 142–168. https://doi.org/10.1177/1075547017696165

McDonald, M. M., Zeigler-Hill, V., Vrabel, J. K., & Escobar, M. (2019). A single-item measure for assessing STEM identity. *Frontiers in Education, 4*, 78. https://doi.org/10.3389/feduc.2019.00078

Michigan State University Provost's Committee on University Outreach. (1993). *University outreach at Michigan State University: Extending knowledge to serve society.* Michigan State University.

Munn, M., Griswold, J., Starks, H., Fullerton, S., Viernes, C., Sipe, T., Brown, M., Dwight, C., Knuth, R., & Levias, S. (2018). Celebrating STEM in rural communities: A model for an inclusive science and engineering festival. *Journal of STEM Outreach, 1*(1), 1–11. https://doi.org/10.15695/jstem/v1i1.4

National Academies of Sciences, Engineering, and Medicine (NASEM). (2016). *Science literacy: Concepts, contexts, and consequences.* The National Academies Press. https://doi.org/10.17226/23595

———. (2018a). *How people learn II: Learners, contexts, and cultures.* The National Academies Press. https://doi.org/10.17226/24783

———. (2018b). *Learning through citizen science: Enhancing opportunities by design.* The National Academies Press. https://doi.org/10.17226/25183

———. (2020). *NASA's Science Activation program: Achievements and opportunities.* The National Academies Press. https://doi.org/10.17226/25569

———. (2022). *Science and engineering in preschool through elementary grades: The brilliance of children and the strengths of educators.* The National Academies Press. https://doi.org/10.17226/26215

———. (2024). *Equity in K-12 STEM education: Framing decisions for the future.* The National Academies Press. https://doi.org/10.17226/26859

National Aeronautics and Space Administration (NASA). (n.d.). About Science Activation. https://science.nasa.gov/learn/about-science-activation.

———. (2022). *NASA Science Activation Impact Report.* https://smd-cms.nasa.gov/wp-content/uploads/2023/02/2022-sciact-impact-report-tagged-1.pdf

———. (2023a). *NASA Science Activation Impact Report.* https://science.nasa.gov/wp-content/uploads/2024/05/2023-sciact-impact-report-tagged.pdf

———. (2023b). *NASA's 2023 equity action plan.* https://assets.performance.gov/cx/equity-action-plans/2023/EO_14091_NASA_EAP_2023.pdf

National Institutes of Health. (2023, September 27). *NIH launches community-led research program to advance health equity* [News release]. https://www.nih.gov/news-events/news-releases/nih-launches-community-led-research-program-advance-health-equity

National Research Council (NRC). (2006). *America's lab report: Investigations in high school science.* The National Academies Press. https://www.nap.edu/catalog/11311/americas-lab-report-investigations-in-high-school-science.

———. (2009). *Learning science in informal environments: People, places, and pursuits.* The National Academies Press. https://doi.org/10.17226/12190

National Science Foundation. (2022). *Leading the world in discovery and innovation, STEM talent development, and the delivery of benefits from research: NSF strategic plan for fiscal years 2022–2026.* https://www.nsf.gov/pubs/2022/nsf22068/nsf22068.pdf

Nielsen, K., Gathings, M. J., & Peterman, K. (2019). New, not different: Data-driven perspectives on science festival audiences. *Science Communication, 41*(2), 254–264. https://doi.org/10.1177/1075547019832312

Nolen, S. B., Ward, C. J., & Horn, I. S. (2011). Motivation, engagement, and identity: Opening a conversation. In D. M. McInnerny, R. A. Walker, & G. A. Liem (Eds.), *Sociocultural theories of learning and motivation: Looking back, looking forward* (pp. 109–135). IAP Information Age Publishing.

Oetzel, J. G., Duran, B., Sussman, A., Pearson, C., Magarati, M., Khodyakov, D., & Wallerstein, N. (2017). Evaluation of CBPR partnerships and outcomes. In N. Wallerstein, B. Duran, J. G. Oetzel, & M. Minkler (Eds.), *Community-based participatory research for health: Advancing social and health equity* (p. 237–250). John Wiley & Sons.

Ostman, R. (2024). *STEM learning ecosystems.* Star Library Network. https://www.spacescience.org/edu/reports/Ostman_BR_FINAL.pdf

Oyserman, D., & Destin, M. (2010). Identity-based motivation: Implications for intervention. *The Counseling Psychologist, 38*(7), 1001–1043. https://doi.org/10.1177/0011000010374775

Pacific Research and Evaluation, LLC. (2021, May). *Portfolio evaluation plan.*

Pandya, R. E. (2012). A framework for engaging diverse communities in citizen science in the US. *Frontiers in Ecology and the Environment, 10*(6), 314–317. https://doi.org/10.1890/120007

Pinkard, N. (2019). Freedom of movement: Defining, researching, and designing the components of a healthy learning ecosystem. *Human Development, 62*(1–2), 40–65. https://doi.org/10.1159/000496075

Shepard, P. M. (2002). Advancing environmental justice through community-based participatory research. *Environmental Health Perspectives, 110*(Suppl 2), 139. https://doi.org/10.1289/ehp.02110s2139

Soleri, D., Long, J. W., Ramirez-Andreotta, M. D., Eitemiller, R., & Pandya, R. (2016). Finding pathways to more equitable and meaningful public-scientist partnerships. *Citizen Science: Theory and Practice, 1*(1), 9. https://doi.org/10.5334/cstp.46

Star, S. L. (1985). Scientific work and uncertainty. *Social Studies of Science, 15*(3), 391–427. https://doi.org/10.1177/030631285015003

Stoecker, R. (2003). Are academics irrelevant? Approaches and roles for scholars in community based participatory research. In M. Winkler & N. Wallerstein (Eds.), *Community-based participatory research for health* (pp. 98–112). John Wiley & Sons.

Teresa, R. M., Valentina, P., Gerardo, A., Cesare, N. M., Roberta, M., Čedomire, Š., Stojanovic, M., Rosi, L., & Gianfranco, D. (2023). Community-based participatory research to engage disadvantaged communities: Levels of engagement reached and how to increase it. A systematic review. *Health Policy*, 104905. https://doi.org/10.1016/j.healthpol.2023.104905

Tuck, E., & Guishard, M. (2013). Uncollapsing ethics: Racialized sciencism, settler coloniality, and an ethical framework of decolonial participatory action research. In T. M. Kress, C. Malott, & B. Porfilio (Eds.), *Challenging status quo retrenchment: New directions in critical research* (pp. 3–27). Pacific Research and Evaluation.

Villegas, M., Sullivan, T. K., Fuxman, S., & Dewhurst, M. (2007). Re-envisioning research as social change: Four students' collaborative journey. *Journal of Research Practice, 3*(1), M7.

Wallerstein, N., Duran, B., Oetzel, J. G., & Minkler, M. (Eds.). (2017). *Community-based participatory research for health: Advancing social and health equity.* John Wiley & Sons. https://doi.org/10.1353/cpr.2019.0022

Wenger, E. (1998). *Communities of practice: Learning, meaning, and identity.* Cambridge University Press.

Yua, E., Raymond-Yakoubian, J., Aluaq Daniel, R., & Behe, C. (2022). A framework for co-production of knowledge in the context of Arctic research. *Ecology and Society, 27*(34). https://doi.org/10.5751/ES-12960-270134

Appendix A

Input for the Committee

SCIACT 2.0 SPEAKERS

1. Kristen Erickson (sponsor), Science Activation, NASA
2. Lin Chambers (sponsor), Science Activation, NASA
3. Kristi Manseth, Pacific Research and Evaluation, LLC
4. Steve Rider, Pacific Research and Evaluation, LLC
5. Taline Kuyumjian, Pacific Research and Evaluation, LLC
6. Ben Hamlington, NASA Jet Propulsion Laboratory
7. Carl Lewis, Fairchild Gardens
8. Sue Allen, Allen & Associates
9. Dennis Schatz, Pacific Science Center
10. Jackie DeLisi, Education Development Center
11. Eric Banilower, Horizon Research
12. Colleen Manning, Goodman Research Group

SCIACT 2.0 SITE VISITS

1. **NASA Principal Investigator Meeting** (Leesburg, VA)—Lin Chambers, SciAct Project Manager
2. **NASA HEAT** (Dallas, TX)—Michael Kirk, Project Director, NASA HEAT—Eclipse week
3. **Exploratorium** (San Francisco, CA)—Rob Semper, Principal Investigator; Robyn Higdon, Co-Principal Investigator
4. **NASA's Neurodiversity Network** (Sonoma State University)—Lynn Cominsky, Principal Investigator

5. **NASA Night Sky Network** (Oakland, CA)—Vivian White, Principal Investigator
6. **Astronomy Activation Ambassadors** (SETI Institute, CA)—Dana Backman, Principal Investigator
7. **NASA Community College Network** (San Francisco, CA)—Simon Steel, Principal Investigator
8. **Gulf of Maine Research Institute** (Presque Isle, ME)—Leigh Peake, Principal Investigator
9. **Native Earth | Native Sky / Choctaw Cultural Center** (Durant, OK)— Kathryn Gardner-Vandy, Assistant Professor, Oklahoma State University (OSU), and Principal Investigator, Native Earth | Native Sky; Juliana Utley, Retired Professor of Mathematics Education, OSU, and Co-Investigator, Native Earth | Native Sky; Sarah McDowell, PhD student in Science Education, OSU, and Graduate Research Associate, Native Earth | Native Sky; Kena Hawkins, Citizen of the Cherokee Nation and Program Coordinator, Native Earth | Native Sky

Appendix B

Committee Members' Biographies

MARGARET HONEY (*Chair*, she/her/hers) is the chief executive officer and president at the Scratch Foundation. Prior to joining the foundation, she led the New York Hall of Science (NYSCI) for 15 years, where she leveraged the museum as a platform for innovation in STEM education and developed NYSCI's distinctive Design-Make-Play approach to STEM learning. That hands-on approach to STEM learning and engagement was infused into everything from Design Lab, one of the largest design and engineering spaces in the nation; to the long-running World Maker Faire that NYSCI hosted, to the Playground Physics app and curriculum; to Connected Worlds, one of the first and largest digitally immersive exhibits in the world. Under Honey's leadership, NYSCI also formed a deep and lasting partnership with families, educators, and other non-profits in the Corona and East Elmhurst communities of Queens, building a science, technology, engineering, art, and mathematics-themed preschool on the NYSCI campus that brings high-quality STEM learning to more than 300 3- and 4-year-olds each year. In addition to her tenure at NYSCI, she also served as a vice president of the Education Development Center (EDC) and director of EDC's Center for Children and Technology. While at EDC, Honey was the architect and overseer of numerous large-scale projects funded by organizations including the National Science Foundation, the Institute of Education Sciences, the Carnegie Corporation, the Library of Congress, the U.S. Department of Education, and the U.S. Department of Energy. She codirected the Northeast and Islands Regional Education Laboratory, a $40 million federally funded initiative designed to help educators, policy makers, and communities improve schools by helping them access and leverage the most current research about learning and K–12 education. Honey has shared what she's learned before Congress, state legislatures, and federal panels, and through numerous articles, chapters, and books. She is a member of the National Academy of Education and serves on the boards of Bank Street College of Education, Post University, and Sphero. Honey received her Ph.D. in developmental psychology from Columbia University. She has chaired multiple National Academies of Sciences, Engineering, and Medicine consensus studies, working closely with the Board on Science Education.

WENDY GRAM (*Vice Chair,* she/her/hers) has worked at the interface of science and education for over 30 years. She is the deputy director of COMET, a University Corporation for Atmospheric Research program. COMET develops education and training products for weather, water, and climate sciences, and provides them freely on the MetEd learning portal. Prior to joining COMET, Gram was the lead for science engagement and education for the National Science Foundation-funded National Ecological Observatory Network (NEON) for 10 years. At NEON, she led development, implementation, and evaluation of education and engagement programs and tools to enable the scientific community to effectively discover, access, and use NEON data. Before this placement, Gram was head of education at the Sam Noble Oklahoma Museum of Natural History at the University of Oklahoma. There, she was a member of the senior leadership team for the museum and led programs that integrated science with educational programming, such as innovative teacher professional development workshops, field courses, K–12 classes, and exhibit development. Gram holds a B.A. in biology from the University of Pennsylvania and a Ph.D. in ecology and evolution from the University of Missouri. She was a member of the 2019 National Academies of Sciences, Engineering, and Medicine's Committee to Assess Science Activation.

FLÁVIO S. AZEVEDO (he/him/his) is associate professor in STEM education, Department of Curriculum and Instruction in the College of Education, at the University of Texas at Austin; and co-director of the UTeach Natural Sciences teacher education program at the same institution. His research focuses on the nature of interest-driven participation in STEM practices, STEM learning in and out of schools, and liberatory pedagogies. Broadly, to speak of people's interests is to consider the multitudinous ways in which diverse individuals engage and appropriate any given practice, so that pedagogies for interest development can be powerful pedagogies for democratic participation. Azevedo investigates interest-driven participation and learning across timescales and settings of STEM practice (hobbies, after-school programs, classrooms, museums, and the home), as well as the sociocultural and political contexts of such practices, so as to broaden and deepen participation in STEM and to intervene on mechanisms that (re)produce inequities across educational spaces. He is a Spencer Foundation fellow and a member of the International Society of the Learning Sciences and the American Educational Research Association, among others. Azevedo holds a B.S. in electrical engineering, an M.S. in computer science, and a Ph.D. in science and mathematics education.

PAULA BONTEMPI (she/her/hers) is dean of the Graduate School of Oceanography at the University of Rhode Island. Prior to her current position, she served as acting deputy director at NASA's Earth Science Division in the Science Mission Directorate of NASA Headquarters, and spent more than 16 years as the physical scientist and program manager for ocean biology and biogeochemistry at NASA Headquarters. Bontempi provided leadership, strategic direction, and overall management for the agency's Earth science portfolio, from technology development, applied science, and research to mission implementation and operations. Her scientific interests include Earth and ocean remote sensing, phytoplankton ecology, marine bio-optics, studying the Earth as a system, oceans across the solar system, the connection of ocean exploration to global economics, and the development of ocean sensors. Bontempi has a strong interest in mentorship and justice, equity, diversity, and inclusion initiatives in science, technology, engineering, and mathematics. She currently serves as a member of the NASA Unidentified Aerial Phenomenon Independent Study Team and is a fellow of the Oceanography Society. Bontempi has a B.S. from Boston College, an M.S. from Texas A&M University, and a Ph.D. in oceanography from the University of Rhode Island.

ORLANDO FIGUEROA (he/him/his) is the founder of Orlando Leadership Enterprise, LLC. Prior to this position, he was a NASA senior executive with 45 years of experience in the management, planning, and development of scientific space programs, missions, and related technologies. Figueroa has experience at the NASA Goddard Space Flight Center and Headquarters including as deputy center director for science and technology, director for applied engineering and technology, deputy associate administrator for science programs, director of the solar system exploration, director for Mars exploration, and deputy chief engineer for systems engineering. He has been awarded the National Space Society Pioneer Award, Smithsonian Latino Center Legacy Award, Service to America Federal Employee of the Year Medal, NASA Presidential Rank Awards, Most Influential Hispanics in the Nation, Pioneer Award from the Hispanic Engineer National Achievement Awards Corporation, NASA Outstanding Leadership Medals, and the Community Stars Award from the Maryland Science Commission. Figueroa has authored publications in the field of cryogenics, the SMEX missions, and the Mars Exploration Program. He received a B.S. in mechanical engineering from the University of Puerto Rico, an advanced studies degree in mechanical engineering from the University of Maryland, and an honorary doctorate degree in science from Dominican College.

ROGERS P. HALL (he/him/his) is Wachtmeister Family Professor of Education, Emeritus, at Vanderbilt University. With colleagues in the Space, Learning and Mobility Lab, he designs and studies learning environments that invite new ways to engage with STEM conceptual practices. These include studies of learning in ensemble and embodied activity (e.g., "walking scale geometry," mathematical aspects of dance choreography), where mobility is both the means and content of what is learned (e.g., youth counter mapping to expand personal mobility), and by making and sharing "story lines" that bridge archival collections, classrooms, and city neighborhoods as a form of public history.

VICTOR R. LEE (he/him/his) is an associate professor in the Stanford Graduate School of Education. His research involves the study and design of science, technology, engineering, and mathematics learning experiences with an emphasis on supporting teaching and learning with data, artificial intelligence literacy, elementary computer science education, and science teaching and learning. Lee's work has traversed formal and informal learning spaces including schools, libraries, homes, and afterschool programs. He is past recipient of a National Science Foundation CAREER Award, American Educational Research Association's Jan Hawkins Award, and a National Academy of Education/Spencer Foundation Postdoctoral Fellowship. Lee sits on the editorial boards of several leading education research journals and is past president and an elected fellow of the International Society of the Learning Sciences. He received a B.S. in cognitive science and mathematics from the University of California, San Diego, and a Ph.D. in learning sciences at Northwestern University. Lee was previously a member of the committee that produced the National Academies of Sciences, Engineering, and Medicine's consensus report *Cultivating Interest and Competencies in Computing: Authentic Experiences and Design Factors*.

ALINA MARTINEZ (she/her/hers) is a former principal researcher at Mathematica and former director for Mathematica's STEM research area. She has over 25 years of experience conducting studies of federal programs funded by NASA, National Science Foundation, U.S. Department of Education, and National Institutes of Health. Martinez has directed and played a senior role in over two dozen studies, including evaluations of STEM education and training programs that extend from middle school through early career, and evaluations of research programs that involve large-scale research center collaborations, interdisciplinary research, and international research experiences. Her work has also investigated programs to promote educational access and success of students. Prior to joining Mathematica, Martinez was a principal associate at Abt Associates. She began her career as a middle school science teacher in the Los Angeles Unified School District. Martinez received a B.S. in biology from Cornell University; an M.A. in educational foundations from California State University, Los Angeles; as well as both an M.Ed. and Ed.D. in education policy from Harvard University.

RAJUL PANDYA (he/him/his) is professor of practice at Mary Lou Fulton Teachers College and executive director at Global Futures Education Lab at Arizona State University. Prior to these positions, he was vice president of community science at the American Geophysical Union. Pandya focused on how the sciences can be more participatory, how inclusivity contributes to innovation and relevance, and how the sciences can be allies in advancing justice. He has served or is serving on advisory boards for the Cornell Lab of Ornithology, Public Lab, the Community and College Partners Program, the Citizen Science Association, the Anthropocene Alliance, the Denver Institute for Science and Policy, ISET International, and the science and research subcommittee for the City of Denver's Sustainability Advisory Council. Pandya received a Ph.D. from University of Washington, which investigated how large thunderstorms grow and persist. He chaired the National Academies of Sciences, Engineering, and Medicine's Committee on Designing Citizen Science to Support Science Learning and Enhancing Opportunities by Design.

DARRYL N. WILLIAMS (he/him/his) is the Franklin Institute's senior vice president of science and education, overseeing core aspects of the mission at the heart of the Institute's efforts to inspire a passion for learning about science and technology. He joined the Institute from Tufts University's School of Engineering where he was dean of undergraduate education and director of Tufts Center for STEM Diversity. Prior to Tufts, Williams spent four years with the National Science Foundation as a rotating program director and managed a range of federal programs and research focused on engineering education, STEM teaching and learning, designing formal and informal learning environments, and workforce development. He earned his B.S. in chemical engineering from Hampton University and his M.S. and Ph.D. in chemical engineering from the University of Maryland, College Park. Williams is a current member of the Board on Science Education and a member of the NASA STEM Engagement Committee.